This book belongs to:

D0112345

FAIR WARNING	BOOK CONTAINS
- Ego Shattering Wisdom	- Irreverent Humor
- Cursing Language	- Loud Rock-N-Roll
- Tequila Drinking	- Life Changing Insights
- Bar Fighting	- Emotional Button Pushing
- Iguanas and Dragons	- High Octane Adventures

R Rated   *PTE* publishing

Badass Awards

Spirituality for Badasses- Book 1
2022 WINNER
New Age

Spirituality for Badasses- Book 1
2022 FINALIST
Spiritual

Spirituality for Badasses- Book 1
2021 1st Place GOLD WINNER
New Age Spiritual

Spirituality for Badasses- Book 1
2021 2nd Place SILVER WINNER
Philosophy

Thanks to all the fans and readers who made this possible. I like awards, but I like changing lives better. — J. Stewart

PLEASE LEAVE A REVIEW !

Make your world a more spiritual badass place: After reading, please leave a review with your thoughts, opinions and stars. You can do so on Amazon, Kobo, Goodreads, Bookbub or Smashwords. Spread the love baby. Thanks and enjoy the ride... - *J. Stewart Dixon*

FAN & READER REVIEWS

I just can't get enough of Spiritually for Badasses! It truly has helped open my eyes and I can't thank you enough! Highly recommend. – **Kim Goetz**

One of few books on spirituality that has successfully held my attention –**Jamie**

Spirituality for Badasses gives you a genuine and realistic approach to spirituality. It gives you a practical and honest guidance towards becoming a spiritual badass by removing the formality and handing you a jolt of awareness. –**Yvette Alvarado**

It is an awesome book and J. answers a lot of life's questions while managing to tell you 'like it is' without fear. He just writes what everyone thinks but is afraid to say on such a touchy topic. –**Loren Gentry**

FINALLY - someone who writes the words to make sense of the madness in my head! Thank you! –**Joanna**

Just want to say....WRITE FASTER I'm almost to page 165 in one sitting! Thank you for this...it's obvious you wrote this JUST FOR ME!... Thank you thank you and thank you! –**Jasmine Martinez**

Thank you SO very VERY much, J!! VERY much appreciated!! And, YES!! Your work not only heals and entertains, but also INSPIRES! Thanks again!! –**Gina C**

I enjoyed the irreverent style and tongue in cheek tone. It has given me some new perspectives on a subject that interests me and I will definitely put them into practice. I look forward to reading the rest. Thank you for the preview! –**Courtney Wilson**

Awesomeness! It really is an enjoyable read and I dig your energy; you're very much my type of person. No holds barred honesty and some funny funny shit. Thanks for being so gracious! I look forward to buying the completed book when you're finished. –**Starr Anderson**

I loved your book. I am an F bomb mom, my spirit animal is deadpool. So, I totally dug it…I look forward to reading the rest of the book. Great job. Thank you for putting it out there. –**Mindy Rabon**

5 STARS all the way! –**James Edward Mack Jr.**

Read right away in one sitting and was blown away. Mostly by the writing style but also by the fact that there is too much fluffy writing out there about (spirituality) enlightenment. I'd rate it Two thumbs and two big toes up. –**Chris Taylor**

PROFESSIONAL REVIEWS

"Spirituality for Badasses should be part of any self-help, spirituality, or mindfulness collection. It goes where no other books in these genres dare travel, doing so … in a way no other book matches."
–Midwest Book Review

"Dixon has much to offer, repackaging mysticism, intentionality, and self-care into something proudly lowbrow and accessible. … A jokey yet earnest and useful guide to enlightenment for badass readers."
– Kirkus Reviews

"(Dixon) has clearly done his spiritual homework and he succeeds at distilling the effective and life-changing ingredients of contemplation and initiation. His relationship to his student/reader is like a shaman drill sergeant cajoling and nudging and ultimately getting his team over the hurdle."
–Pacific Book Review

"It's this shedding of typical, formalist intonations and the possession of a good sense of fun that makes Spirituality for Badasses, along with J. Stewart Dixon, entertaining – but never at the expense of holistically sharing material. That's to be commended."
–The Magic Pen

"In his new book, *Spirituality for Badasses*, J. Stewart Dixon has written an irreverent, exuberant, free-wheeling, stream-of-consciousness saga that chronicles the spiritual journey in ways that are unique, humorous, challenging and a hell of a lot of fun. Buckle up and be prepared for a wild ride that's readable, accessible and eminently relatable. Two enthusiastic thumbs up! Highly recommended!"
–Chuck Hillig, Licensed Psychotherapist, Spiritual Teacher & Author

"Spirituality for Badasses is *The Way of the Peaceful Warrior* for the rebels among us who are tired of sickly-sweet approaches to spirituality and have a sincere need to laugh out loud on the regular.

J. Stewart Dixon is a true original … He's your irreverent, potty-mouthed best friend and big brother, but don't let the humor fool you: the teachings offered here are profoundly liberating, important pointers to awakened awareness. Dixon teaches us all to en-LIGHTEN-UP with his special blend of hilarious, profound, crazy-ass wisdom."
–Erin Reese, M.S., Spiritual Counselor, Teacher & Author

"Accessible. Compulsive. Irreverent. Fun. Practical. All the while lacking nothing in richness or depth.

Take an adventure with J - a spiritual guide that comes off more Han Solo than Obi Wan Kenobi on the surface - as you journey along with the R-rated spiritual everyman with a lizard draped over his shoulders on a path that winds inside and out, through valleys and up mountains, volcanoes and earthquakes, as you make your way toward becoming more your badass true aware self. This book is rich!"
–Zac Cannon, Pastor

SPIRITUALITY
for
Badasses

HOW TO FIND INNER PEACE & HAPPINESS
WITHOUT LOSING YOUR COOL

J. Stewart Dixon

PhE
publishing

V 2.0   2022

ISBN: 978-0-9858579-0-5 (Paperback)

Cover design by J. Stewart Dixon & Darren Wheeling
www.blackegg.com

Edited by Mary Lib Morgan
www.perfectlypenned4you.com

PIE Publishing
Charlottesville, VA
www.spiritualityforbadasses.com

Contents

PART 3: The Ninja Warrior Jedi Mindfulness Trick

PART 4: Ego's Your Bitch

How to be open minded without being a flake

Okay, you can relax.

Here're some ground rules I think you'll appreciate:

There will be nothing–zero, zip, nada–written, channeled or prophesied in the pages of this book concerning the following:

- No pious exhortations, hostage demands or icy cold Gansta threats for you to join a church, organization or online cult.

- (With the exception of *The Weekend Warrior Knitters Club* at the local Moose Lodge #45. Joining this club is absolutely mandatory.)

- No meditation marathons, daily four-hour zazen practices, extreme yoga postures or sitting on a pillow until your ass-cheeks fall off from boredom and/or stiffness.

- No reincarnation, past lives, or attempts to contact your dead aunt Martha (Leave your poor Aunt Martha the fuck alone)

- No crystal energy, vortices, chakras, lay lines, galactic

- energy shifts or Edgar Cayce prophecies concerning the volcanic demise of Atlantis or the Chapter 11 of Blockbuster Video.

- No disincarnate entities, channeling, ghosts, zombies, moth men, aliens or any creature (corporeal or otherwise) mentioned on the X-Files.

- No gurus, devotion, religious rituals, new age ceremonies, hippy sweat lodges, mantras, chants or Starbucks coffee aromatherapy enemas (too damn expensive).

- No non-duality, Neo-Advaita Vedanta , *You're already this, that and the other thing BS,* quotes from the *Bhagavad Gita,* or the combined media mogul teachings of Eckhart Tolle and Oprah.

- Finally- no, No, NO! We are NOT going discuss, talk, whisper, write, channel, or scream during sex anything about: The Law of Attraction, The Secret, manifesting your soulmate or how to use spirituality as your personal cosmic ATM machine.

- (If you figure the ATM shit out, please send me the details.)

How to be a badass without being a badass-hole

I get it. I really do.

You're a badass.

Cool, hip, down-to-earth, together, sane, practical, tough, smart, confident, fringe, alternative, creative, funny, athletic. However, you want to quantify your badass-ness.

You've been this way your whole life, or maybe it took a couple of decades for you to cultivate it, or maybe it just kicked in yesterday at 3:09 pm. Who knows…and who cares, right?

Because something is missing.

It seems that being a badass just isn't—enough.

Is it?

Let me make this easy for you. I'm also a badass…

…except that for most of my adult life I've been involved with spirituality. And maybe you can relate here—this badass has always had…um, a slight issue: He doesn't really love spirituality, being spiritual or hanging out in spiritual circles.

No thank you.

This badass…well, eh... he loves beer.

There—I said it! I love beer. Dark beer. Craft beer. Locally brewed beer. I also love fly fishing and kayaking and hiking in the mountains. I love making fart jokes with my twelve-year-old son. I love smoking the occasional cigar (or other things) in my hot tub. I love great sex. I love head massages. I love making lots of money. I love cool cars. I love taking vacations in tropical places. I love hanging out with friends and being potty mouthed. I love watching Netflix. I love sitting around on the weekends and doing absolutely nothing. There are a lot of things this badass loves.

But spirituality? No, I don't love spirituality.

But...I do like it. I really like spirituality—a lot.

Spirituality has served this badass well. Here are a few of the benefits I gained from my years involved with spirituality:

- I used to be depressed. I am now depression free—because of spirituality.

- I used to be deeply unhappy most of the time. I am now happy most of the time—because of spirituality.

- I used to be unaware and off balance about lots of things. I am now very aware and mostly balanced about lots of things—because of spirituality.

- I used to be a mindless idiot caught, obsessed and jerked around by the thoughts in my head. I am now a mindfulness master who realizes that the thoughts in my head are mostly irrelevant, neurotic and frivolous—because of spirituality.

- I used to be timid. I used to avoid conflict. I used to deny certain emotions. I am now outspoken, unafraid of conflict, and I fully embrace all emotions whether they feel good or bad—because of spirituality.

- I used to believe that all existence was a flat, one dimensional, dead end. I now know from repeated experience that life—existence—is a multi-layered, vibrant, and mysterious realm—because of spirituality.

- I used to believe that death meant the end. I now know, also from repeated experience, that death is not the end and some part of us continues—because of spirituality.

- I used to believe that who I was was this separate individual named J. Stewart. I now know that the real me springs from this same timeless, limitless ONE that we all are—because of spirituality.

So you see...I really do get it. I used to be depressed, anxious, too smart for my own good, opinionated and unhappy...a real loveless badass-hole. But now I'm just a spiritual badass.

Spirituality removed the hole. I transformed. I changed. I grew up. I learned some hard lessons. And I did all this without ever losing my cool, integrity, smarts, libido, sense of humor or soul. And that's just what this book is going to help you do.

You and I are going on a road trip, starting in my hometown and then traveling across the United States. Along the way, we'll visit some amazing places, take a few high-risk adventures and experience some strange shit. But what we're really doing is exploring and where we're really going is into the vast uncharted territories of your deepest soul.

Will it be easy? Nope. Will it be uncomfortable? Yep. Will it shake your world up like a three-hundred-foot drop on a Six Flags roller coaster? I hope so.

But you're a badass and can handle this shit, right? Hell, yeah.

> "Come to the edge," he said.
> "We can't, we're afraid!" they responded.
> "Come to the edge," he said.
> "We can't, We will fall!" they responded.
> "Come to the edge," he said.
> And so they came.
> And he pushed them.
> And they flew."
> — Guillaume Apollinaire

Okay. You've now read the introduction. Quit fucking around. Buy the book and let's get started.

Fist bump,

J. Stewart

J. Stewart Dixon
Charlottesville, VA
www.spiritualityforbadasses.com

P.S. - I like to curse and I curse like a drunken sailor in this book-mostly creatively, for emphasis, authenticity and humor. If you don't like or are offended by cursing, this R-Rated spiritual book probably ain't for you. Thanks.

PART 1

Your Attention Please

CHAPTER 1
ATTENTION

How to pay attention without being a suck-up

Mr. Kim, my high school senior physics teacher, was pissed. He had been painstakingly conveying the details-

Oh wait—

Shit. Sorry.

Brakes on, please.

Gently. That's it.

Thaaank you.

Now steer the car over to the side.

Excellent. Thanks again.

Take a deep breath.

Awesome.

So, before we continue down this road, fall head over heels in love, and end up drunk in a Vegas chapel…whaddya say we pause for a minute and I'll explain how this book works? I'm a pretty sensitive schmuck and was already feeling your anxiety hit the roof.

How!? Huh? What?

So…calm down, now. Here's the scoop:

There is no right way or wrong way to read this book.

There is no memorization required while reading this book.

Just read. Stuff that jibes with you is probably going to stick out like a Porsche 911 GT2 at a Kansas tractor show. Conversely, stuff that does *not* jibe can be thrown into the *Don't Give Two Shits About* trash can.

There will be pit stops, pauses and interruptions…like this one.

You can read this book like you'd Netflix binge a season of *Game of Thrones*…in one Saturday night. Or you can micro-read it in hundreds of ten minute bite-sized portions. Don't matter.

I've laid this book out in a fashion where most chapters build upon the previous chapters: I do *suggest* you read it sequentially, but I won't be offended if you skip around.

Them's the rules.

In short…relax, read, have fun and trust your captain. I've made arrangements with the gods of potty-mouthed spiritual self-help to make sure you get *exactly* what you need.

So, let's get back on the road: All good spiritual road trip adventures begin with…attention.

Okay. Now, where were we? Oh right, Mr. Kim….

Mr. Kim, my high school senior physics teacher, was pissed. He had been painstakingly conveying the details of a mathematical formula when I unleashed the contents of my smart-assed, unfiltered, teenaged mind. "Why bother!?" I blurted out. My epiphany was not what Mr. Kim wanted to hear in that moment; the justifiable tirade he launched into went on for about ten minutes. I learned my lesson—sort of.

It wasn't that I didn't care; I just didn't see the point. Mathematical formulas had seemingly *zero* to do with my life. I just could not summon the enthusiasm to care or pay much attention.

That episode epitomized most of my high school years; I was a mediocre to decent student whose attention span was just good enough to get Bs. I had not found my *true* attention yet.

In spirituality, cultivating attention is the first thing to be done. I'm not talking about the kind of paying attention the teacher told you to do. I'm also not talking about the kind of paying attention that little Suzie Smith, Girl Scout, class president and ass-kissing teacher's pet regularly doles out.

I'm talking about the kind of paying attention used when your hand is on fire and the rest of you is about to go up in skin melting flames. *Badass paying attention.*

Simply put, you must place your attention on the very thing that invited you to open this book in the first place—however minor: anxiety, depression, frustration, suffering, unhappiness, lack of meaning, angst, something's missing, etc. (Of course, paying attention to this shit is exactly what most people—yeah, you included—loathe to pay attention to the *most*.)

So, the first of many uncomfortable truths you will encounter here is this: We're all ostriches—heads buried deep in the sand

and, eventually, we all have to pull our ostrich like chicken-shit heads out of *that sand* and start paying real attention.

My hand's on fire? What hand? What are you talking about?

Exactly.

We're going to help you work on badass attention for the next few chapters.

When I arrived at Syracuse University for college, predictably, I continued down the same inattentive path, until I realized my own *hand on fire* situation: I had contracted a profoundly serious case of long-term depression.

Not a fan of shrinks or pharmaceuticals, I opted for the road *very traveled*—marijuana and manifestos. I smoked a little pot. I read a few books. I earnestly began investigating the world's wisdom traditions, philosophies and religions. I read whatever spiritual books I could get my anxious, depressed hands on and, oddly enough, my true attention was born. I remember the exact moment:

I was taking a Spanish literature class during my sophomore year. We were reading *Don Quixote* by Miguel de Cervantes, and during this class—probably for the first time in my entire academic life—I was paying *complete* attention.

I was enrapt.

I raised my hand for every question.

I spoke up.

I debated.

I paid absolute true attention

because…

I had a personal stake in the subject matter of the book. It wasn't abstract. *It was about me.*

It was about my own battle with the windmills of depression. I, too, was "The Ingenious Nobleman Sir Don Quixote of La Mancha." A lightbulb had gone off in my head—all the stuff written in this book and a hell-of-a-lot of other books was pertinent *to me*. It really mattered, so naturally…*I wanted to pay more attention.*

You're going too fast.

Can we pull over again?

I know—I'm being an annoying prick.

Pull over again. Thanks.

Listen, here's the thing: I want to help you, but I can't when you're doing that shit.

What shit?

Right. Well, the shit you've always been doing: running on automatic and going too fast.

I know, I know—you just want to read the book and enjoy it and maybe learn a little sumpin' and move on…and that's the problem. It's the same old same old. I mean really—how many self-help books have you read that *truly* fucking helped you!?

Well, Jack, not on my watch.

I've realized the trick to a self-help book is to infiltrate it with, well…another self-help book. And so that's what we're gonna do here. We're gonna interrupt that shit you're always doing. Or to be more specific…we're going to interrupt that shit *your mind is always doing* so we can reveal something amazing that precedes it. Okay?

Cool. We'll go over the whys and hows a little later.

For now, let's help you with your speeding.

Do this: Take an honest-to-goodness big breath. Inhale through your nose; fill your chest cavity with air and release.

Do it now.

No. Don't keep reading. Pause and do it.

Right.

Now.

Breathe.

Ahhh…much better. Thank you.

I think this is sufficient for now.

Okay, you can put it back in drive.

Spiritual Badass Lesson:

So I was telling you about my time in college when my true attention was born—Thank you, *Don Quixote*. The lesson I learned at the time (and your first spiritual badass lesson) was/is this: *Reading spiritual shit is good for you.*

When we read spiritual, philosophical or (gasp!) religious books, they expose us to an archetypal "bigger picture" of life. When we begin to see this bigger picture of life and how we fit into its grand scheme, things get personal.

When things get personal, we automatically pay more attention to them. We begin to notice that this "bigger picture" of life has been screaming directly to us all along from everywhere. Literature, science, art, philosophy, religion, math, history and music all contain elements which point to the bigger picture of life—*to you and me right here and now: Hey man, doing the Hokey Pokey is NOT what it's all about. This is who you are. This is what you are capable of. This is how to achieve it. This is where life is headed.*

But here's the ass kicker: Quite often it is our suffering, pain, angst, depression, lack of meaning, and/or unhappiness which kick us in the ass and motivate us into action and into paying more attention: *Hey Dumbass! If you'd just see the bigger picture here, you might stop suffering.*

When we do all this stuff—read a little, see the bigger picture, and cultivate a more courageous and unwavering level of attention, the whole thing kinda snowballs wildly until we become super bona fide spiritual badasses.

And that's exactly what we're going to help you achieve.

For the next few chapters, we're going to examine three destructive patterns which block our "bigger picture" attention: *Lying, Denial and Distraction.* Then we'll place our attention on four key "bigger picture" areas: Our life, our emotions, our thoughts and our body.

Of course, along the way I'm also going to interrupt your lazy, speeding ass and smack you into the present moment. No, friend—this is not *Chicken Soup for the Soul.* This is a double shot of LSD-laced, jalapeño infused Patron tequila…and it's going to eat your soul for breakfast. Just kidding—sort of.

Move along…this chapter has ended.

CHAPTER 2
LYING

How to be honest without being spineless

Sarah N. really depressed me. She lived in the same dormitory as me during my freshman year of college. She was catty, insipid and vindictive. She lived and acted on the surface of a swirling sea of lies and petty activity. And she took every opportunity she could to insult me for who knows what reason. She and her circle of friends provided the first cracks in my worldview, which led to my depression. I quickly concluded that this place, this Earth, this society and this life... *sucked.*

My depression began when I realized that most people like Sarah were caught in a petty matrix of lying, grasping for material success, and denying the inherent struggle and suffering of life. And even worse than realizing this was realizing that I, too, was guilty. I was a petty, lying materialist.

Today I can thank Sarah and her milieu of friends for seeding my depression. It was soon thereafter that I began investigating spirituality, psychology and religion as a means of finding some sanity in the world and in myself. I soon discovered that lying was a ubiquitous human trait.

Okay...so brakes on gently.

Pull over—there.

Awesome…it even has a good view.

Okay, cool.

So—before you get into the next little section, I want to take a moment to do some explaining.

The next section is about *science and research*. And for some of you, this will be a welcome breath of fresh air. Because, I mean—how do you know I'm not pulling all this goomba straight out of my ass? Right?

And for others…*yeah, what-evs. I believe you. No need to science me. I'm a believer.*

Right, so both of you can shut the hell up. You *both* need this.

Because, actually…there's just *one* of you here.

I'm speaking to the two halves of your brain right now. And, throughout this book, I will continue to speak to *the two halves of your brain*. The right brain will usually say *yes* to all my street talkin', potty-mouthed story-telling. And the left brain will usually say *yes* to all the "sciencey" stuff…even if the right brain slightly objects and finds it boring.

And just a teensy side note here: If *you* are aware of your right brain and *you* are aware of your left brain, then who is the *you* being aware? Something to ponder. (For astute readers— yeah you caught me. I was foreshadowing a point that *seems* trivial or inconsequential, but is actually profound as fucking shit.)

So, Mr. Street-talking Right Brain—shut the fuck up, calm down, smoke a doobie and/or take a few more deep breaths and get your science on. In the long run, this is going to provide

some   much-needed   stability,   groundwork   and
logic for your whole crazy spiritual process.

Awesome. Okay.

Now…let's get back on the road.

We were talking about *lying*.

Here's the science:

In 2004, Cornell University psychologist Jeff Hancock and two
of his graduate students, Jennifer Thom-Santelli and Thompson
Ritchie, conducted a research experiment to find out just how
much we lie. They asked 30 students to keep track of their social
communications (face-to-face, telephone, text and email) for
seven days, noting when they lied and how the lie was
transmitted.

Their research determined that 37 percent of telephone
communication, 27 percent of face-to-face communication, 21
percent of text messages, and 14 percent of emails contained
lies.

That's a lot of pants on fire.

Another 2004 research study about lying was conducted by
psychologist Bella M. DePaulo, PhD, from the University of
California, Santa Barbara. DePaulo and her colleagues
questioned 147 college aged and non-college aged participants
about the details of any lying activity throughout the course of
a week.

Most participants reported lying several times per day.

These results provide us with a small glimpse into our ubiquitous predisposition and capacity for lying.

In fact, according to University of Toronto Child Development Psychologist Kang Lee, PhD, lying is an important mental and behavioral milestone in child growth. Lying demonstrates *theory of mind*—the ability to differentiate between what is going on in one's own mind and someone else's mind. Lying also demonstrates executive functioning—the ability to regulate one's behavior and actions.

The bottom line is this: We all lie and lying isn't necessarily good or bad. It's just part of being human.

But, concerning *attention*, it's an aspect of ourselves we cannot afford to sweep under the rug. Understanding and paying attention to our lying unlocks a greater internal vista, which then creates space and possibility for healing, change and growth.

Most of us engage in two types of lies: external lies and internal lies.

External lies

With external lies, we lie to others: our relatives, parents, husbands, wives, children, boyfriends, girlfriends, co-workers, strangers at the coffee shop and even our doctors or priests.

- There are white lies which we use with good intention and to avoid conflict: *That dress looks beautiful on you, dear. My boss is demanding and overbearing, but I respect and admire him.*
- There are ethical lies which we use for the greater good: *There is no money in our vault, Mr. Bank*

Robber. I know karate and kung-fu; back off, Mr. Mugger.

- There are cultural/social lies which we use to please others: *Santa will deliver your toys tomorrow night, dear; he will come down the chimney. Sparky has gone to doggy heaven, dear.*

- There are lies of omission often used if we are in the public eye, media or politics. *I did not have sexual relations with Ms. Lewinsky. Iraq has weapons of mass destruction. There was no quid pro quo.*

- There are bald-faced lies which we use to get attention: *Three days ago, I hunted down and captured Bigfoot. I'm related to the president of the United States.*

- There are fabricated lies which we use for exaggeration purposes: *I ran a marathon and won the lottery yesterday. I make half a million dollars a month.*

Internal lies

With internal lies, we lie to ourselves:

- There are lies of denial which we use to falsely comfort and delude: *I'm fine. Everything is okay. It will all be good soon. Everything is hunky-dory. Nothing wrong or bad here.*

- There are lies of fantasy which we use to mislead ourselves, comfort ourselves and refuse reality: *If I stay positive, think positive and act positive, everything will be positive.*

- There are lies of blame which we use to avoid accountability, responsibility and ownership: *There's nothing I can do. It's not my fault. I'm not to blame. It's his (or her) fault.*

- There are lies of unworthiness which we use as a means of avoiding the challenges of true growth and transformation: *I'm not good enough. I'm not worthy. I'm not capable. I'm not qualified. I'll never be good enough until I have or become this or that.*
- There are lies of the martyr which we use to justify our isolation, loneliness and refusal to live, work and play with others: *If it weren't for me, nothing would get done. I'm the only one who can solve this. I'm a saint. I'm a martyr.*
- There are lies of the misfit which we also use to justify our isolation, loneliness, and refusal to live, work and play with others: *I don't fit in. I'm special. No one else has this problem. I'm all alone.*

Evolutionary biologists have theorized that the behavior of lying arose shortly after the development of language. Lying was simply and necessarily an evolutionary advantage. Lying, manipulation, and coercion required a lot less energy and fewer resources than physical force.

But like all evolutionary developments, this particular advantage has run its course and reached its limit. Lying no longer serves our higher development and is preventing our evolution rather than enabling it.

The cumulative effect of all this habitual internal and external lying is our partial and fragmented attention. If we chronically manipulate and bend the truth, our attention simply cannot sustain a cohesive force or clarity. Greater attention demands greater honesty.

Spiritual Badass Lesson:

As much as we can, we must stop lying to ourselves and others—whether white lies or whoppers. Doing so will strengthen our attention and provide us with a vital tool used in becoming a spiritual badass.

Try to pay attention to your lying. First notice it, then own up to it. Finally, try your hardest, to end it: Stop exaggerating, stop telling half-truths, and stop hiding stuff from others and yourself. If you are unhappy or unsatisfied about something, stop pretending that it's all hunky dory. Confront the situation. Do something about it. Take action. Grow a pair. But do not bury it, hide from it, or pretend it doesn't exist. *Stop lying*. It no longer serves your highest spiritual badass interest.

So... I'm a bit of a mind reader.

And right now, my psychic mind-reading teleportation powers are telling me what you might be thinking:

Should I believe this guy?

Should I trust this guy?

Who the fuck is this guy, anyway?

He's kind of funny, but can I really take his self-help spiritual advice seriously?

I get it. I totally do.

Here you are, driving around in a car with a stranger you just met.

He's making *you* drive, no less.

And he's pontificating and proffering advice about spiritual shit.

Well, duh! Yeah, you should be a little skeptical.

Your thoughts are justifiable.

Nope, no need to pull over.

Keep on driving.

We're headed toward those mountains over there.

Thanks.

Here's my response:

You are correct. I am an unusual and rare bird. For whatever reason, I do not play by the usual nice, calm, spiritual guy or gal rules. Don't be fooled by my irreverent humor, however. My advice is deadly serious.

Credentials?

Sure…

I was a suffering, depressed, anxious fool for decades. Then I weaved my way out of that paradoxical torture maze…using the exact advice and methods offered in this book.

While on my own spiritual road trip, I met and interacted with heavyweights in the spiritual world: Robert Monroe, Yogi Bhajan, Adi Da, Gangaji, Ram Dass, Andrew Cohen, Arjuna Ardagh and Saniel Bonder…to name a few. I even saw the

Dalai Lama live in concert if that means anything to you. He rocks.

I've studied Mindfulness-Based Stress Reduction and Mindfulness-based Cognitive Therapy, both online and at the University of Virginia. Although I must admit, I found these courses rudimentary compared to the depth of my interactions with the spiritual individuals listed above.

For about a decade, I taught mindfulness and spirituality locally and online. I helped a considerable number of people, but grew tired with the business end of the shtick, which was like busking to homeless people in the Mojave Desert. Yeah, um, I have a mortgage to pay. I like money.

I own and operate Audio Video Services LLC, an audio-visual design and installation firm, which has always done well. I'm no right-brained snowflake. I've done work for the U.S. Army, Sears & Roebuck, Wendy's, Hershey's, American Legion, N-Telos and many others.

Last, but not least, I've been married for close to twenty years and have a son who is, as I write this, twelve years old. My family can attest to my potty-mouthed irreverent spiritual humor: Much to the delight of my son and chagrin of my wife, I fart regularly while meditating and occasionally leave the toilet seat up in the bathroom. I'm no saint.

Okay. *Holy Nut Buckets*: I feel like I'm running for president. To quote *Babe's* Farmer Hogett, who was filled with gratitude and happiness for winning the top prize at the county fair..,

"That'll do, pig; that'll do."

How to embrace your shit and not run from it

Alright, turn down that small country road and then follow it all the way to the top of the hill.

I want to show you something.

Turn left up here.

Great.

Okay, park over there.

Let's get out.

Walk with me.

Thanks.

Let's go up here and take in the view.

These are the Blue Ridge Mountains.

Nice, huh?

Actually, I brought you here because I thought this might be a good place to share a story:

Take another deep breath.

Pause. Okay.

A long time ago there were two priests who lived and ran parishes in the same region. For years, the two priests belonged to the same religion; prayed to the same God; and followed the same set of holy words. Both parishes had an equal amount of loyal and devoted followers.

One late spring day, a major earthquake struck and devastated the region, killing hundreds and causing deep untold suffering which impacted the denizens of the area for many years.

Both parishes experienced great loss and hardship. Over the years, each parish had the task of rebuilding. During this time, a very odd thing happened.

One of the parishes thrived and was once again supported by many in the region. It soon built up its attendance to pre-earthquake levels and even surpassed them, resulting in the need for a bigger church. There was a shine to the parish and a glow to all those who attended.

The other parish languished. Only a handful of the most faithful attended. The church grew in disrepair and a solemn black cloud seemed to hover above it. Those who attended had the same solemn look.

The priest of the languishing church heard rumors of the thriving church and, in desperation, paid the other priest a visit. The two priests sat down to tea.

"How? How is this possible?" asked the first priest.

The second priest responded "We changed. Before the earthquake, our church was just like yours...celebrating only the light, the good and the positive. After the earthquake we started down the same path, but soon realized that the damage and trauma of the earthquake ran too deep. So—we changed."

"But how?" The first priest once again implored.

"Very simply," replied the second priest "We stopped celebrating the light…"

The first priest gasped in shock. The second priest continued.

"And we started celebrating *both* the light and the dark. Both life and death. Both pleasure and pain. Both happiness and suffering."

"But the holy words…"

"…were wrong," interrupted the second priest. "For a long time, celebrating only the light served us well. But the times have changed."

"I offer you this last bit of advice," continued the second priest.

He then gathered a small piece of parchment paper and a pen and proceeded to draw a funny looking circle split in two halves, one light and the other dark. The dark half contained a dot of light. The light half contained a dot of dark. He handed the parchment to the first priest.

"Take this…" he said. "To deny death is to deny life and to embrace death is to embrace life. We call it the Tao."

The first priest accepted the parchment paper with the Tao sketched on it and departed. Within a year his parish, too, was thriving and happy.

Good story, huh? I just wanted to share that with you.

Before we get back on the road, pause for another bit, stretch out and take a few deep breaths.

I'll meet you back at the car.

Howdy. Cool?

Let's get on the road again, shall we?

And let's talk about *denial*...

During the first half of my junior year I was studying abroad in London, England. By then, my depression had taken deep root and my search for a solution had turned into a full-scale quest. One weekend, I was exploring with some friends when we happened upon a mini indoor psychic fair. Laughingly, we all sauntered in with egos rivaling the size of Big Ben. There were a variety of booths and vendors. One particular vendor, L. Ron Hubbard's Scientology, invited us to take a free personality test. Jokingly, we all acquiesced. It took me about twenty minutes to fill out the questionnaire and another ten minutes for them to tally the results.

I was not pleased with the results for two reasons: One—L. Ron Hubbard's Scientology is a big, dumb cult that, to this day, I wouldn't touch with a thirty-foot pole. Two—I was in utter denial of what the report said. I have to give Scientology some credit here. They have mastered the basic principles of human psychology and marketing.

Here's what the report said: You're a loner. You're deeply unhappy. You're an angry person. And you're going to be in trouble unless you course correct this now; and naturally, to do so, you should join Scientology immediately.

Except for the joining bit, they were right on all counts: I was a loner. The friends I had been hanging out with that day eventually disappeared. I was definitely unhappy, although at the time I was unwilling to fully own up to this. I was angry about life and my place in it. And yes, I was heading for trouble if I didn't course correct. All of it was true. But I walked out of that psychic fair in a laughing, egotistical state of hard denial. *Not me!* I said to myself. *Not me...*

It would take another two or three years of dropping into deeper depression for me to come to terms with the cold hard facts of my unhappiness, anger and loneliness. Denial does not often unravel quickly.

A little science about denial...

In 1974, Ernest Becker, a cultural anthropologist and PhD from my alma mater, Syracuse University, was awarded the Pulitzer prize for his book *The Denial of Death*. Far ahead of its time, *The Denial of Death* intimately examines the works of Sigmund Freud, Kierkegaard, Otto Rank and Carl Jung. His critique allowed Becker to proffer his own poignant hypothesis about the nature of man: Beyond sex and religion, the fundamental driving and motivational force of our lives is *death*, which we then vehemently deny. Here's a little of what Dr. Becker has to say about this denial:

"The prison of one's character is painstakingly built to deny one thing and one thing alone—one's creatureliness. The creatureliness is the terror. Once you admit that you are a defecating creature, you invite the primeval ocean of creature anxiety to flood over you. But it is more than creature anxiety, it is also man's anxiety; the anxiety that results from the human

paradox that man is an animal who is conscious of his animal limitation."

If we understand the ramifications of what Dr. Becker is saying here, we can comprehend the roots of our situation and become equipped to cure it:

To be human is to naturally contain a certain amount of fear, anxiety, terror and stress. It is an existential part of our nature. However, when we deny or lie to ourselves about this, we create a wall or damn that, over time, builds in pressure, tension and stress. This pressure, tension and stress either slowly leaks or erupts in all sorts of emotional ways: unhappiness, depression, anxiety, meaninglessness, fear, hatred, anger...to name a few.

This existential pressure, tension and stress—this *pain*—is quite natural and okay. There is nothing wrong with it. There is nothing good or bad about it. What *is* wrong is our denial of it. When we deny our existential pain, we cut off or stifle a completely natural part of our own humanity. When we deny our existential pain, it greatly sabotages our truest attention.

The standard medical definition of denial is as follows:

a psychological, unconscious and primitive defense mechanism in which confrontation with a conflict, painful feeling, personal problem or with reality is avoided by denying the existence of the problem or reality.

Denial is our lizard brain telling us to look away as a means of protecting ourselves. Short term, it works quite well. Long term—it's a disaster.

There are three basic types of denial: existential, cultural and circumstantial.

Existential denial covers the big topics: fear, death, suffering, anxiety, limitation, childhood wounds, body, emotion, thoughts, survival, struggle, insignificance, meaning and depression.

Cultural denial covers the basics of who we are: race, skin color, body form, feminine nature, masculine nature, sexuality, status, class, education and intelligence.

Circumstantial denial covers our day to day life circumstances: loneliness, loss, bad relationship, abuse, dysfunction, addiction, sickness, health, opinions, likes, dislikes, pleasure and pain.

Spiritual Badass Lesson:

Exposing denial and then placing our attention on that which we have been denying is Spiritual Badass Kung-fu. It's the gateway into reclaiming lost parts of our humanity, sanity and happiness.

As evidenced by my personal anecdote, it's not necessarily easy...but it is possible. Knowing that it is possible and developing the courage and fortitude to proceed is where we begin.

We should also acknowledge that our denial has served us, protected us and saved us. But its service, as shown in the story of the two priests and the Tao, is now outdated and no longer required.

The most effective way to meet and dissipate denial is with compassion, caring and understanding. Three basic things you can do to dissipate denial: One—Select something you may be in denial about. Two—Write out the details of the denial in a letter to yourself. Three—Confide in someone about it.

As we continue our adventure together we'll learn more tools like awareness and mindfulness, which will assist us in reducing the denial habit. By seeing denial, placing our *attention* on it and letting it go, we can move on to a greater, freer, spiritual badass possibility.

CHAPTER 4
DISTRACTION

How to put your cell phone down for one goddamn minute

A couple of years after college I became aware of the deep existential level of distraction that all human beings carry around in their psyches. After college, my investigation into all things spiritual, psychological and religious kicked into high gear. I had taken up a transient lifestyle, living and working in a variety of states from New York to Texas to California. I owned a small library of classic philosophical and spiritual books. I had met with various teachers, authors and guides. I had been to workshops, classes and private sessions.

All of this inner reflection, study, experience and travel had a profound effect on me. I became a self-contained laboratory and my mind was the guinea pig. Slowly I began to understand its machinations, and slowly my attention became fierce and courageous. I was willing to focus on anything.

One night during the intensity of this time, I awoke at about three a.m. trembling to my core with chills and feelings of dread. I was having a full-on existential anxiety attack. I had reached rock bottom. I had finally, completely pulled back the *Wizard of Oz* curtain charade that was my ego and mind. Now exposed, I could see it clearly. There, cowering in the corner, was my outdated lizard brain. I couldn't unsee this shit:

The ancient lizard portion of our brains (which, for most of us, retains dominant control) is wired for *existential distraction.*

43

Human beings are distraction machines. Our outward behaviors distract us. Our emotions distract us. Our thoughts distract us. Our desires distract us. Our dreams distract us. Our entire ego and personality structures are built from the ground up to *distract us*. Most of us have no clue how deep the brain's distraction rabbit hole really goes.

And here's the part I will never be able to unsee: My ego finally saw itself. It was like peering over the event horizon of a black hole into a swirling vacuum of raw, unfiltered fear, death and annihilation. My lizard brain had been exposed and foiled. Its primary job—to distract and keep the illusion of a separate ego-I-you alive at all costs—had been completely seen and threatened.

Believe it or not, I was able to reassemble myself and, after a few days, went back to life as usual. After realizing the depth of existential distraction in my own psyche, I returned home and found it on display in my friends and relatives. It was when I saw this deeply ingrained distraction in my family and friends that I knew I had crossed a threshold from which there was no going back. It crushed me. All human beings are existentially distracting themselves…constantly. It was an amazing insight and a terrifying one.

Today when we mention distraction, it's a no-brainer in the next breath to mention smartphones, iPads, televisions and then perhaps material objects such as fast cars and fast food, and then alcohol and drugs. These are all easy forms of distraction to recognize. We live in a world where the possibility of endless distraction is bought, sold, recommended, advised and expected.

According to Alex Pang, Ph.D., a visiting scholar at Stanford University, there are three types of distraction: hijacked, aimless and wandering.

Hijacked distraction is where we should be paying attention to A but then our attention is captured by B and we veer off-course and pay attention to B instead. Our smartphones are a classic example of the B that hijacks our A.

Aimless distraction is classically what Buddhists call "monkey mind." This is where our attention should be on A, but instead it's unfocused and all over the place—on B, C, G, F, L, and Z.

Wandering distraction is the best of the three because we aren't trying to focus on anything (A or B) and we are allowing our minds to wander in a creatively restorative and beneficial way.

Noticing and understanding these three common types of distraction is a good start. Spiritual badass warriors however go one step further: We do battle with existential distraction.

Existential distraction, subtly and profoundly hard wired into the root structures of the ego-mind-personality, is the glue which holds the illusion of the separate ego-I-you together. It's hard to see because it doesn't *want* to be seen. Extract yourself however from its sticky infinite web and your attention will know—no boundaries.

Spiritual Badass Lesson:

We can't escape surface level distraction and it is neither good nor bad. Some distraction, like a wandering mind, is beneficial. However, if we wish to get to the root of our depressed, unloved, unhappy, anxious, fucked-up parts, we must discover a level of *existential distraction* which is created and controlled by the ancient lizard portion of our brains. Exposing it gives us the power and freedom to consciously shift our attention away from its imperative—to exist at all costs— and toward the freedom and happiness we are longing for.

Oh right—your cell phone.

Um. Okay...we can't do this while driving.

There's a pull-off in about a mile.

They're everywhere here on the Blue Ridge Parkway.

Ahhh...okay, great.

Another spectacular view.

Look at that drop off!

You have your smartphone...yeah?

Of course you do.

Come over here to the edge with me.

Alright.

You know what happens now…right?

You delete all social media apps from your phone —Facebook, Twitter, Instagram, whatevs—entirely.

What!? You thought I was gonna ask you to throw your phone over the cliff!

Ha!

By that horrified look on your face, you'd think deleting some silly apps was the same as chucking the whole phone over the cliff!

You wanna be a spiritual badass?

Delete those apps, baby.

Delete those apps!

And you know *exactly* why.

CHAPTER 5
LIFE

How to grab life by the horns and ride it like a space cowboy

---

A teacher of mine once said something like this: Hold up a thimble and the whole ocean can pour over your head, but you're still only going to get a thimble's full of water. Regarding the bigger picture of life, its meaning, and our place in it... most of us are holding up thimbles. Most of us are dying of thirst.

It's getting dark...which is perfect.

In about a mile, there's another overlook.

We'll stop there and hike up a bit.

It'll be pitch black by the time we get to the good part.

And that's perfect.

Pull over here.

Beautiful.

Oh, here—I brought flashlights.

Just follow that path over there.

See you at the top.

If I were owner and operator of a planetarium or a telescopic observatory, it wouldn't be named some boring ass name like *Thomas Jefferson Astronomical Observatory* or *William Barr Smith Planetarium*. No Ma'am. I'd call it what it should be called: *The Mind Fuck Star Gazing Academy*. I'd throw in the word *Academy* because that has a nice ring to it and I'm a big fan of Star Trek which, as every good Trekkie knows, is home to *Starfleet Academy*.

I'd call it *Mind Fuck* because, yeah, that too has a nice ring to it, but mostly because that's what looking at the stars should be all about. They should fuck with your mind.

But of course, most people don't really look at the stars. In our thimble-holding culture, we tend to gaze upon the stars in the same sleepy-eyed, comatose way we gaze upon cows in a field; or upon that half-empty roll of double-ply toilet paper in the master bathroom; or upon the cat vomit on the sidewalk that Sylvester puked up in the middle of last night. Yeah, we really don't look at the stars—much less in a way that blows our fucking minds.

Whaddya say we change that?

Cool. Glad you made it.

So now that you're here with me at the top of this mountain in the pitch black...take a gander at that shit, would ya?

Holy Mother of Mary! Have you ever seen a more beautiful, awe-inspiring sight than that!?

The Milky Way!

My God, I want to lick it! I want to mind-meld it into the soul of my very being. I want to swim in the swirling depths of its breathtaking beauty. I want to drown in its mystery! I want to collide with the smithereens of its infinity.

Oh, great LORD of mystery—*will you look at that!*

It is an orgasm for the eyes.

It is a masterpiece. It defines the very word and transcends it simultaneously.

The Milky Way.

It cannot be touched or had or bought or sold.

Yet it is available for all to behold and hold and, alas, even hold at bay.

I am humbled before its majesty and might.

I am centerless.

I am boundaryless.

I am humbled.

I am...

I am...

I am...

Happy. Small. Big. Infinite. Full. Empty. Rich. Poor. Amazed. Dazzled. Humbled.

All this...just by looking at the stars.

Oh, *the stars...*

I am wobbly-kneed.

Hold my hand.

Thank you.

That—my friend,

...is how members of *The Mind Fuck Star Gazing Academy* look at the stars.

That was amazing!

Pause.

Breathe...

Are you ready?

Let's get back to the car.

I suggest you take a few deep breaths before continuing.

One Saturday night during my freshman year of college, I found myself depressed, alone and bored. My roommate had gone out of town and left me the keys to his Jeep Wrangler So I borrowed it and drove.

I didn't drive with any particular destination in mind. I headed north, vaguely toward Canada. My only agenda was to drive—*and think*. I always found thinking while driving therapeutic and relaxing, probably because the *act* of driving gives the left brain something to do, freeing up the right brain to daydream and fantasize. I enjoyed it.

So I drove and drove, and I thought and thought. I can't say I remember the specific contents of my thinking—but I do remember the gist of it:

What the fuck am I doing here?!?! Why the fuck am I here?!?! Who the fuck am I?!?! Yeah, well, not exactly the thoughts of a wizened sophisticate, but something like that.

I eventually ended up pulling off on a back road and driving out into a field and staring up at—you guessed it—the stars. I remember wishing some aliens would pity-abduct me but it never happened, so I drove out of the field and headed south back to school.

We can begin to build our *bigger picture* muscles by asking bigger picture questions. *Who am I? Why am I here? What is my purpose? (Will I ever get one of those alien guest star gigs on Star Trek?)*

Perhaps we are reticent to ask such questions because we believe they are more appropriate in the church or the meditation hall. Or perhaps we have never considered them at all. Either way, neither belief nor disbelief is required to ask.

We aren't necessarily looking for direct answers either, although they may indeed arrive. The benefits of asking bigger picture questions manifest as the capacity to live beyond our small, isolated egos while embracing life in a larger context. Placing our attention on these "bigger picture" questions turns thimbles into canyons. I have noticed that much of our depression, unhappiness, anxiety and fucked-upness has a very difficult time sustaining itself...in canyons.

Take a few moments to read and reflect on the following questions. Allow time between each question for an answer to arrive...or not. After you've done this, take it a step further: Pick a couple of questions, write them down, and log your answers.

Spiritual badass questions about life:

- Who am I?
- Why am I here?
- What is my purpose?
- How is my life?
- Am I happy with my life?
- Am I living the life I desire?
- How are my relationships with my family and friends?
- What kind of person am I?
- Am I being the kind of person I desire to be?
- Am I treating others the way I desire to be treated?
- Am I fulfilled and engaged with everyday activity?
- Is my work or career rewarding and fulfilling?
- Is there anything from my past I am avoiding?
- Is there anything today I am avoiding?
- How is my relationship to society at large?
- How is my relationship to the earth and nature?
- Am I happy, fulfilled, and satisfied?

Spiritual Badass Lesson:

If you are holding onto your thimble and thirsting for meaning, do this: Pick a clear night, travel to the country, and behold the night sky—no telescope, no phone, no guides or books or instructions or labels. Simply using the naked eye, take your time, look up and allow the baffling infinite mystery of the firmament to sink in. If you really allow it, it's a humbling experience because you are not separate from the infinite mystery of the stars: You are an integral part of it.

Connecting to the bigger picture of life is something your unfulfilled spiritual badass is calling you to do. Instead of blaming our life circumstances, brain chemistry, or childhoods, we may do well to examine the thimbles we are holding up. Ask big questions and see what happens. What have you got to lose?

Fun facts brought to you by *The Mind Fuck Star Gazing Academy:*

Space is big: 1 Light Year =5,903,026,326,255 miles. The Milky Way Galaxy is 105,700 light years wide.

Space is old: The universe is 14 billion years old. Our solar system is 4.57 billion years old.

You are old: Every atom in your body was created by exploding stars billions of years ago.

There are a lot of stars: There are more stars in space than there are grains of sand on all the beaches, parks and sandboxes in the world. To be exact, there are 1 septillion stars; that's 1 with 24 zeros after it...and this is a low estimate.

Space is silent: Sorry Star Wars and Star Trek nerds- not a single *pew-pew* laser blast or hyper-drive is audible in space.

Outer Space is close: It's just 62 miles above your head right now.

You can time travel: When you look at the stars you are looking back in time, because what you are seeing is not the actual star. You are seeing the star light that took millions of years to reach you. The actual star is probably all grown up by now.

You can't burp: Carbonated drinks will never be served on connecting flights to Mars because, in the absence of gravity, you can't burp. I know...bummer, right?

CHAPTER 6
EMOTION

How to stop being an emotional iceberg

The extent to which we will go to avoid emotions is astonishing. An acquaintance of mine, James, served two tours of duty in Iraq. He served as a communications liaison foot soldier who went door to door on resident status checks with a contingency of five to six other soldiers in downtown war-torn Kabul. Frequently his small group would be met with fear and hostility. On numerous occasions they were met with suicide bombers. Somehow James survived these two tours, but he didn't do so without being deeply affected.

In order to do this type of work, most soldiers are trained vigorously to "harden up," bottle their fear, and swallow their emotions. This is completely understandable training given the nature of their work. The battlefield is no place to display or process emotions. James was no exception to this rule.

Of course, what happens to most soldiers is that after the training, the tour of duty, and the war are over—they are left emotionally stunted and debilitated. James confessed that he was more capable of running into a battle zone with bombs dropping, machine guns firing, and glass shattering than he was of confronting and processing his own emotions. So, when James returned home from Iraq for the last time, he spent years unpacking and dealing with all the emotions he had suppressed.

We all suppress and avoid our emotions to one degree or another. The battlefield of life throws us plenty of reasons to avoid or suppress our emotions: abuse, neglect, trauma, illness, unexpected change, death of friends or family. We learn from an early age that emotional suppression and avoidance are often our only means of protection. But, as with my acquaintance friend James, this protection often comes at a high cost. When we suppress or avoid our emotions, it's like we're paying for something with a credit card. Sooner or later, we're going to have to pay off that balance—and usually with high interest.

To continue with this analogy, often our depression is telling us that our credit card is maxed out. No one feels good or is happy about a maxed-out credit card. Attention, then, is the currency we can use to begin to bring the balance down. Our goal at first is to get out of debt, so we must apply our attention to those emotional areas which have long been ignored or neglected. Once the balance has dropped to a healthier level, we can practice the artful skill of paying attention and processing our emotions moment to moment, accruing no more debt.

Take a few moments to read and reflect on the following questions. Allow time between each question for an answer to arrive...or not. After you've done this, take it a step further: Pick a couple of questions. Write them down and log your answers.

Spiritual badass questions for emotions:

Are you open to feeling and experiencing any of these emotions?

- Peace, joy, ecstasy ?
- Trust, admiration, love ?
- Apprehension, fear, terror ?

- Surprise, amazement ?
- Pensiveness, sadness, grief ?
- Boredom, disgust, loathing ?
- Annoyance, anger, rage ?
- Acceptance, guilt ?
- Elation, depression ?
- Superiority, unworthiness ?
- Confidence, shame ?
- Humility, boastfulness ?
- Balance, exhaustion ?

When was the last time you strongly experienced any one of these emotions?

How did you like experiencing it / them?

Which emotions do you avoid?

Which emotions do you overindulge?

Like many of you, I had a lopsided definition of spirituality in my mid-twenties. It lopped toward the bright and beautiful. Spirituality, meditation, yoga, spiritual books, smokin' a spliff with incense burning, whatever. It all represented one kind of thing: Gettin' high, feelin' good, catchin' a buzz, becoming happier and shinier. Even "enlightenment" really meant just one thing: some kind of eternal self-masturbatory Dr. Feelgood oneness with everything. Yeah, I know. Looking back—the whole thing was a little sleazy.

Little did I know that true badass spirituality started with shadow and darkness—or coming to terms with all the shit we don't want to come to terms with.

I first learned this lesson when I was in my mid-twenties.

A friend was visiting one weekend. She was much better at emotional processing than I was. For God knows what reason, while sitting on the couch with her that day, my waterworks started pouring about something I never would have associated with spirituality...my sister.

Damn if I wasn't crying like a baby and simultaneously feeling all this strange buzzing energy coursing through my body. My friend helped me understand that I was experiencing the release of a long-held emotional block that had been created years ago with my sister.

I love my sister and our relationship today is much better, but she would heartily attest that we are very different people. This difference was natural, but it widened when I went off to a private boarding school and she stayed in public school. This created a rift between us that never fully healed.

And here it was, demanding to be reckoned with on that couch when I was twenty-seven years old. I cried and cried and cried at the loss of my pal, friend and emotional equal—my sister. I missed our relationship...the innocent one of the seven and nine-year-old. Where had my little sister gone?

Tears streamed and I shook violently as cascades of energy unfolded, released and opened up.

Afterwards, I was a bewildered slab of raw meat. But simultaneously I was also wide-eyed, happy and at peace. I remember thinking *What the fuck was that?*

What I had just experienced was one of the true fruits of spirituality: the body-mind release of long-held emotional baggage. (It's also called dealin' with yer karma, dawg.)

Damn—it was powerful! And it forever changed my definition of spirituality.

Spiritual Badass Lesson:

In practical terms and in service toward becoming a spiritual badass, what this means is that we must be willing to meet the "bigger picture" of our emotions. Unchecked, they become long overdue, unpaid credit cards burdened with toxic fees and penalties. However you can, pay that shit off right now and get rid of the credit card.

The best course of action is to take a good hard look, accept and ultimately release any stifled, hidden or blocked emotional content. How do you do this? The most effective way is to find a shoulder to cry on. Find someone you trust—a friend, relative, teacher, counselor, coach or therapist and let-r-rip.

Yes, this takes a little practice, time, trust and courage, but your badass self will thank you (and with the money you save on your credit card you can get a big ol' iced-double-mocha-latte at Starbucks.)

CHAPTER 7
THOUGHTS

How to deal with the crazy person in your head

A famous parable about thought goes something like this:

Two monks were walking down a wooded path and arrived at a stream. At the stream's edge was the local prostitute; she pleaded to be carried across the stream so her dress wouldn't get wet. The first of the two monks obliged. She hopped on his back. All three crossed the stream. After crossing, the prostitute headed toward town and the two monks headed toward their monastery. After some time on the path, the second monk finally broke down and exclaimed:

"How could you do such a thing!? Carrying that immoral woman on your back!"

The first monk, looked at the second and replied:

"I'm no longer carrying her, but you—it seems—still are."

All of us carry around thoughts and thought patterns. We try to avoid some thoughts and, like the second monk in the parable, assign them false importance. We obsess and ruminate unnecessarily about others. Our outdated lizard brains are endless thought generating machines. When we can see this, our obsession, compulsion, denial and avoidance of thoughts relax.

Again—here's the trick: Honest, clear and courageous attention on thoughts increases our capacity to see those thoughts, to allow them and embrace them. The challenge, once again, is to replace thought thimbles with thought canyons. Attention is the tool used to do this.

When we become canyon-sized, no thought or thought pattern can disturb, irritate or depress us. Thoughts are free to come and go; then we are freed from the pain and unhappiness they cause.

Take a few moments to read and reflect on the list of thoughts and thought patterns below.

Actually, eyes on the road. Keep driving.

Okay...look. I know, I know.

Holy fuck! Look at that long list of shit he wants me to read.

And there it is: Thought Pattern #456,762 ...

I hate reading long lists of shit.

Fair enough, but suck it up.

At the very least I want you to get one thing out of this list— and it's this:

YOU are not the things on this list.

YOU are the one who observes and is aware of the list.

These are just a bunch of bullshit thoughts generated by that brain nestled in your head.

YOU are not them.

That's the point of the list and the exercise.

Understood?

Cool.

You got this.

Spiritual badass negative thoughts to notice:

- I'm not there yet.
- When I get this or that, I'll be…
- I'll be happy when…
- I hope I get the…
- I can't do it.
- I can't get it right.
- I'm a failure.
- I'm not successful.
- I'll never understand.
- It'll never happen to me.
- I'm not good enough.
- I'm not smart enough.
- I don't deserve it.
- I'm too old.
- I'm too young.
- I'm not rich.
- I don't have enough.
- I'm not pretty.
- I'm too heavy.

- I don't feel like...
- I wasn't born with...
- I'm not talented enough.
- My life sucks.
- I hate life.
- Why does life have to be so…
- Why me?
- Bullshit.
- Fuck you.
- Fuck me.
- Fuck everything.
- Fuck this place.
- This is hell.
- What a shithole.
- God damn it.
- Are you fucking kidding me?
- There's not enough time.
- Why is this taking so long?
- I'll be here forever.
- I don't want to go to...
- I hate this.
- I want more meaning in...
- I'm damaged.
- I'm depressed.
- I'm sad.
- I'm lonely.
- I'm empty.
- I'm unhappy.
- I'm afraid.

Spiritual badass positive thoughts to notice:

- Wow, that was..!

- What fun that...
- What a beautiful...
- It was an amazing...
- I'm very grateful.
- We loved...
- I like...
- I'm very fond of...
- She's a very...
- He's a very...
- I love...
- I'm excited for...
- Delicious!
- Awesome! I get a...
- I'm capable of…
- I can do...
- I got this.
- I want to try.
- Sign me up.
- I'm not afraid of…

Spiritual badass thought patterns to notice:

- *Reading Minds:* He thinks I'm a loser. She hates me.
- *Predicting the future:* I'll fail that exam. I won't get that job.
- *Catastrophizing:* I won't be able to pay the mortgage. We'll be out on the street.
- *Negative labeling*: I'm undesirable. He's a rotten person.
- *Discounting positives:* Those successes were easy, so they don't matter. She's supposed to cook dinner, so her efforts don't count.
- *Seeing only negative:* No one likes me. Another crappy day.

- *Comparison:* She's more successful than I am. He's better looking than me.
- *Overgeneralizing:* This always happens to me. I fail at everything.
- *Exaggeration:* Everyone rejects me. It was a big waste of time.
- *Shoulds:* I should do well. If I don't, then I'm a failure. I should get a raise.
- *Personalization:* My marriage ended because I failed at...
- *Blame:* She's to blame for the way I feel now. My parents caused all my problems.
- *Regret:* I could have won if only I tried harder. I shouldn't have said that.
- *What if:* What if I make a mistake? What if I'm not good enough?
- *Victim:* There's nothing I can do to change it. We're just pawns in their hands.
- *Judgement:* He's smarter than me. She's successful. I'm not.
- *You're responsible*: It's my fault you're not happy. I can make you happy and a better person.
- *You see fairly:* I see what is reasonable and fair and you don't.
- *Change others*: If I can just get her to change she'll be happy.
- *Always right:* I know I'm right and I'll prove it to them.
- *Fantasy Rewards:* After all this hard work I deserve recognition, success, and reward. Why the hell wasn't I rewarded after all that hard work?

I have a confession to make. Because, man—if I can't confess, then how can I expect you to? Alas... I must lead by example.

So here we go:

In 1981, shortly after I had entered boarding school in the eighth grade, a devious thought pattern entered my mind that would plague me for the rest of my life. It had to do with a girl.

Now, I don't want to give you the wrong impression here: this was just normal puberty related sexual fantasy stuff; the kind that every pimply boner-infected 14-year old boy experiences at this age.

But man—I must've really grinded that shit deep, because the staying power of that thought has astounded me throughout the years. I shit you not...as I write this, I am fifty years old and I still have dreams about that girl.

And trust me...I am waaaay over that girl, but I gotta give credit to the staying power of that thought pattern. Thoughts can be devious and tenacious little bitches.

The point here is that we all carry around thought patterns. My brain does what my brain does—and I am okay with it. I am quite well aware that I am more than my brain. Who I am is not defined by the thoughts in my head. Nor am I at war with the thoughts in my head.

And so I confess: Even us pros have to deal with thought patterns...some of them quite old. They're just a fact of life and part of the pros and cons of having a cerebral cortex. The heart pumps blood. The lungs breath oxygen. And the brain thinks thoughts.

Who I am and who you are in the most spiritual badass sense of the word goes way beyond the brain. And that is some good news...no matter what you think about it.

Spiritual Badass Lesson:

There's one quick and easy way for you to get a little distance between the crazy person in your head and the real you—and you already know how to do it:

Breathe.

The S.T.O.P. method is commonly used in Mindfulness-Based Stress Reduction courses. We've been practicing it a little bit already.

There are four steps, one for each letter:

S.T.O.P.

Stop

Take a breath

Observe

Proceed

Super simple. Super effective.

Try it the next time some crazy ass thought is buzzing around inside your head.

CHAPTER 8
BODY

How to get over it and accept that you've got one

The tag line for the 2018 Amy Schumer comedy film *I Feel Pretty* is "change everything without changing anything." In the movie, Amy Schumer's character bumps her head after falling off an exercise bike and goes from feeling bodily unworthy and ashamed to feeling bodily worthy and beautiful.

I don't know too many people who, at some time or another, haven't wished for a bump on the head to rid themselves of bodily shame, unworthiness or guilt. Instead of the magical cure offered in the movie, however, most of us opt for the next best method: avoidance.

It's no surprise, then, that the last "bigger picture" item we need to devote our attention to is the body. Our bodies are often starved for attention.

The attention we need to give our bodies, however, is not the attention sold by slick Madison Avenue advertising companies in the form of stylish clothing, hair gels, weight loss programs or any of an infinite number of surface methods or products.

Au contraire mon ami. We need to see, accept and pay attention to our bodies just as they are in this moment. We need to pay attention to our naked, imperfect, always changing, growing and dying bodies.

71

Our bodies are sending us messages all the time. Often when we are depressed, unhappy or anxious we tend to avoid these messages, because they are either too painful or too numerous to deal with. Either way, we tend to numb over, avoid and shy away from these bodily messages.

The *thimble-canyon* analogy works here as well. How many bodily messages are we capable of receiving and paying attention to? You'd be surprised.

The way we increase this capacity is to simply do it. The challenge is to take the first step and then the next and the next—until we are no longer holding our attention back from our bodies. Our bodies will thank us and the long-term reward is that the stream of unhappy, depressing messages it sends slowly dries up.

Now, I want to take you some place I think your *body* is going to like…

I hope you've enjoyed our brief tour of the Blue Ridge Mountains yesterday.

Oh, and thanks for driving again today by the way.

Why don't I drive?

Yeah…good question.

Because you should be responsible and empowered. This is *your* hero's journey. I am not here to save you. You save you. I don't drive out of deep respect for your adventure.

Okay, that being said—let's pull over here..

Where we're going is...sacred ground.

Monacan Indian sacred ground to be exact.

It's down here near the river—the Rivanna.

Follow me.

What I want to show you and why I want to show it to you has to do with your body.

Just a little more.

Okay, here we are.

Pause...

Take a deep breath.

Pause again.

Take another deep breath.

Now...place your attention on your feet and legs.

Not much to see here, is there?

This place is called the Monacan Mound. The mound eroded into this flat field long ago. But an Indian burial mound was here for over a thousand years. Thomas Jefferson discovered it. Thousands of native American human beings were buried peacefully...right here.

Pause.

Take a deep breath.

Notice your feet touching the earth.

Oddly enough, I didn't know this was a burial ground until just a few months ago...but my body knew it years ago. I've been fly fishing here for over a decade, and I kid you not—I had no clue this area was an Indian burial ground.

But my body did.

Every time I walked by this spot—and I walked by it over a hundred times— something in my body relaxed, deepened and felt sacred. My body knew. And that's the point of showing you this spot.

Most people think spirituality is about escaping the body, going within and experiencing some sort of vast inner subtle realm. You know—meditation, enlightenment, heaven, out-of-body experiences, near-death soul travel, whatever... stuff like that.

And I'm not denying any of that—if this kind of thing is your cup of tea.

But damn if there isn't a whole other ball game level of spirituality that has everything to do with *being in* the body and living in the sacred present moment.

Your body knows.

Right now, for instance, because we're here in this sacred place, you may notice something going on in your body:

Your body is experiencing a stillness.

Your body is experiencing a deepening.

Your body is experiencing a calm.

Your mind is settling.

Your feet, legs, arms and extremities are feeling lighter.

Your breathing is deepening.

Your peripheral vision is expanding.

Your heart is opening.

Your body is smiling.

You are smiling.

And there you have it.

Your first glimpse of Badass Spirituality.

A little inner peace and happiness...all without losing your cool.

I'm going to let you hang here in this space for a bit.

Take a few moments.

Then read the questions below. The point of these questions is not to change or improve the body. The point is to pay complete attention to the body. Allow time between each question for an answer to arrive...or not. After you've done this, take it a step further: Pick a couple of questions. Write them down and then log your answers.

Spiritual badass questions for your body:

- Is your body in any pain?
- Is your body feeling pleasure?
- Is your body stressed ?
- Is your body at peace?
- Is your body irritated?
- Is your body hot or cold?

- Is your body achy ?
- Is your body agitated ?
- Is your body restless ?
- Is your body fidgeting ?
- Is your body comfortable in its own skin?
- Is your body accepted?
- Is your body rejected?
- Is your body loved?
- Is your body hated?
- Is your body beautiful?
- Is your body ugly?
- Is your body healthy?
- Is your body receiving proper nutrition?
- Is your body receiving enough exercise?
- Is your body overweight?
- Is your body skinny?
- Is your body weak?
- Is your body strong?
- Is your body constantly exhausted?
- Is your body full of energy?
- Is your body feeling good?
- Is your body feeling bad?
- Is your body ill?
- Is your body damaged?
- Is your body in need of repair?
- Is your body working properly?
- Is your body young?
- Is your body old?

Spiritual Badass Lesson:

Maybe you've heard all the spiritual hoopla about living in the present moment or the "power of now"? It's an often talked about and of course, insanely over-hyped spiritual truth. Experiencing the unfiltered present moment for long periods of time can indeed be a profound experience. (Non-hyped truth: Most of the time it just feels normal or natural) Either way- I highly recommend it. I have no doubts that if you stick with me here you too will eventually catch a glimpse or a good long stretch of it.

Well, guess how you get there?: *The body- your body.*

Your body resides exclusively in the present moment. *Your body* knows no past or future. So yes, paying attention to your body is an important part of becoming a spiritual badass. *Your body* is the gateway to the present moment. Go figure.

Here's a super simple body exercise that will cost you a few bucks, but is completely worth it: Go get a professional massage. Book at least an hour-long appointment for a Saturday morning if you can; then spend the rest of the day relaxing, listening to and *paying attention* to your body.

This isn't just a feel-good exercise. This is you intentionally getting in touch with the *present moment.* Many of us have a hard time relaxing because our bodies are so wound up with all the usual life stress, toxins and bullshit. Getting a massage instantly cuts through that bullshit and realigns your body –with the present-spiritual-badass-now.

END PART 1

Continue your adventure with J.:
Connect, share, laugh, grow & learn
with other books, articles,
videos, courses & more...

Go here:
www.spiritualityforbadasses.com

PART 2

Aware of Awareness

CHAPTER 9
EVOLUTION

How to evolve from a suffering badass-hole to a spiritual badass

On December 27th 1831, a sailing vessel with a crew of seventy-three men sailed out of Plymouth Harbor, England on an expedition that would circumnavigate the globe for five years. The ship, humbly named the H.M.S. Beagle, carried a passenger whose scientific research would forever change how we viewed the natural world. The passenger's name was Charles Darwin and his book, *On the Origin of Species*, was published nearly thirty years after this famous voyage. Darwin's theory of natural selection proposed a branching tree of life from which different species could share a common ancestor.

Darwin didn't just crack the code of evolution; he brought it out of the dark ages and defined it. The world's living species— plants, animals and human beings— evolve.

Today, what is very odd about Darwin's theory is that we seem to have forgotten something vital. Our collective somnambulant malaise has brushed off one very cogent aspect: human beings are still evolving.

If you take away only one thing from *Spirituality for Badasses*, let it be this:

You are still evolving—and the driving force of that evolution is a yearning for something more or something better. Let's just call it *existential yearning*.

Existential yearning is none other than the natural force of evolution itself. It can be subtle, presenting itself in the form of curiosity, questioning or doubting. Or it can be severe, presenting itself in the form of pain, suffering, depression or meaninglessness. Either way, it's usually experienced as a lack or a hole or a missing of something.

So, your next obvious question should be:

Okay, what is the *something* that is missing?

That is an excellent question.

Here's the answer:

Oddly enough and simply enough...it's awareness.

Yep. Evolution sayeth unto thee: *Hey dummy, notice awareness and see what happens.*

I know this sounds odd. All our troubles can be solved with awareness? Huh? Are you kidding me?

Nope—I am most definitely not. Stick with me and you'll understand.

It goes without saying that humanity as a whole has definitely *not* noticed awareness. We have instead noticed the lack and we have declared war on the lack. Using every conceivable weapon under the sun, we have done our mightiest to kill the lack, drug the lack, numb the lack, hide the lack, deny the lack, fuck the lack or eat the lack. You get the idea:

antidepressants, opioids, pornography, money, fame, prestige, power. The list is endless.

I know, I know. It sounds like we're all fucked, but we're not. Here's why:

The counterintuitive paradoxical badass solution to lack is this:

You ready?

You can't kill the lack.

You can notice it. You can pay attention to it. You can accept it. You can embrace it. You can even love it if you want to. But you cannot kill it, get rid of it or eliminate it. Never, ever.

You can only do what evolution is asking you to do: Become *aware* of the lack and *evolve* it. This whole book and the road trip adventure we're taking together *is all about evolving your lack—with awareness.*

If you can understand and pay complete attention to this idea, you will fulfill your particular existential yearning and *evolve the lack*—not by ignoring it, resisting it, drugging it, numbing it or stopping it—but by cooperating 100% with it and learning from it.

Here's what you can learn: *Lack* is actually a precious gift from evolution. It's what drives you to evolve and what drives you to be more aware.

I know it doesn't seem possible right now, but trust me when I say that fully developed awareness is a mighty thing, capable of taming—not defeating—the mightiest of dragons.

Awareness is the only thing that can transform and change the lack.

Allow me to *Star Wars* this shit. It's actually pretty simple: How does Luke Skywalker finally save Darth Vader?

He doesn't kill him. He doesn't damn him for all eternity. He doesn't even hate him forever.

He simply forgives him, accepts him and embraces him. Darth Vader—the very definition of darkness, evil and *lack*—is saved by Luke's forgiveness, acceptance and love.

And that's as mushy as this book is gonna get.

May the force (of awareness) be with you.

Hey!

You awake, sunshine?

I totally forgot to tell you yesterday!

Today we are going on an *epic adventure* to one of my favorite spots!

And we are going in *style…*

This, my friend, is the newest Wrangler Limited Edition 4x4 Off Road Jeep.

Hell yeah, it's chartreuse!

My favorite color.

Give me a minute to pull down the top.

It's a gorgeous day.

Here; take the keys.

Ready to go?

Put it in drive…

The badass *aware you* is gonna love this!

What makes it epic?

Well.

eh—

It's fucking dangerous… :)

You drive.

I'll babble.

Over time, I came to see my own existential yearning *manifested as depression* not as a flaw to be drugged or numbed but as an invitation from evolution itself:

Wake up, Dumbass…you're still in a cocoon! No wonder you're unhappy. It's dark and cramped in there. Get the hell out of that thing!

Giving my attention to and accepting this evolutionary invitation was one of the best decisions I've ever made. It ended my depression and it fulfilled the yearning.

Once I gave my attention (ala Part 1) to this yearning, I began to notice something very particular about attention: It's tethered to and integral to something slightly bigger…*awareness*.

The relationship between attention and awareness is like an arrow. Attention (which you *already* have) is the pointed end of the arrow and *awareness* (which you also *already* have) is the fletching feathered end of the arrow. You can't really separate the two, but they can indeed and quite often do become out of balance.

Most people are clueless—out of balance— regarding the full potential of awareness: It's usually unnoticed, taken for granted, or conceived of as just a small part of the functioning brain. But snoop around a bit, and you'll discover that awareness is pretty damn amazing and a lot more important than you would ever have expected.

Okay—brakes on.

Slow down a bit. You're speeding.

Let's S.T.O.P.

Stop.

Take a breath.

Come on now—really do it.

Observe.

Proceed.

Much better...

This is how you really use a self-help book to make a change.

So, if I were a smart self-help author, I'd segue into a section right about now that has to do with the science of awareness. I could spout all sorts of statistics and research and quotes from famous neuroscientists using fancy terms like neuroplasticity, neurogenesis, triune brain, mirror neurons and what not. And I could impress you with my own personal research into the science behind awareness, including courses I've completed at the University of Virginia's Mindfulness Center.

But fuck, man, *the truth of the matter is this*: Science doesn't know jack-shit about consciousness or awareness.

Take a second to feel into and recognize that empty space behind the eyes in your head, apparently located in the brain. Now, before there are any thoughts about it, before labels, before scientific knowledge, before spiritual intuition or whatever, ask yourself *What or who is that? What is awareness?* And if you answer honestly, you'll say "It's a mystery, a complete and utter mystery."

Indeed, neuroscience has discovered quite a bit about the brain—everything from neuroplasticity to mirror neurons to being able to map the active or inactive regions of the brain through fMRI. But they haven't discovered the consciousness neuron or synapse or the awareness cell or the consciousness-aware molecule. There are lots of theories about interconnectivity and thought, but no tangible definitive answer to what awareness is—how it's generated or where it comes from.

But don't take my word for it. Here's what a 2019 article by Shelly Fan of the Allen Institute for Brain Research in Seattle, Washington says about the origin of consciousness:

"How physical systems give rise to subjective experience is dubbed the 'hard problem' of consciousness. Although neuroscientists can measure the crackling of electrical activity among neurons and their networks, no one understands how consciousness emerges from individual spikes. The sense of awareness and self simply can't be reduced down to neuronal pulses, at least with our current state of understanding."

An older Scientific American research article titled "A Theory of Consciousness" by Christof Koch (2009) states roughly the same thing:

"The truth is that we really do not know which of these organisms is or is not conscious. We have strong feelings about the matter, molded by tradition, religion and law. But we have no objective, rational method, no step-by-step procedure, to determine whether a given organism has subjective states, has feelings.

"The reason is that we lack a coherent framework for consciousness. Although consciousness is the only way we know about the world within and around us...there is no agreement about what it is, how it relates to highly organized matter or what its role in life is. This situation is scandalous! We have a detailed and very successful framework for matter and for energy but not for the mind-body problem...."

So, there you have it. Another uncomfortable truth: There will always be some part of spirituality and, consequently, *you* that is forever shrouded in mystery.

A teacher of mine used to call it *divine ignorance*. Get used to this idea. It's a badass idea. You will never figure it all out and even if you could...who cares?

I seriously doubt knowing that awareness arises from the synaptic firing of the meta-carpus-neural network complex buried in the sub-angulus-cortical center of the prefrontal lobe hemisphere would make you any goddamn happier.

And yes, that last sentence was a fictional load of alphabet cat-vomit. You're welcome.

Spiritual Badass Lesson:

Pay attention to your own particular style of evolutionary yearning and lack. Try to get in touch with this yearning and lack and become clear about it. How does it manifest? How often does it show up? Can you hear it faintly or loudly? How do you currently answer it? Write the answers to each of these questions down. Review, re-ask and re-write weekly until you are completely clear about your own yearning and lack.

This is super important: This is your particular invitation from evolution. The more you pay attention to it, the clearer it becomes and the sooner you can evolve it...with awareness.

Accepting mystery as part of this process is something you should get used to. The mystery of awareness is, in many ways, like the mystery of the stars. There's a lot we know. But there's a hell of a lot more we don't know. Mystery is badass. The sooner you get comfortable with it, the better.

All this talk about awareness. You just might be wondering:

So how do I get some?

That's another very good question. Happy to oblige.

But first, we're going to stop for lunch.

Keep driving. GPS says another five miles down this road.

I packed some tasty treats.

We're almost there.

CHAPTER 10
NOTICING SHIT

How to notice shit with your eyes,
nose, hands and tongue

So right up here is the entrance. Pull over in front of that gate.

Awesome.

Thanks.

I've gotta unlock the gate. Gimme a sec...

Okay, we're all set.

You cool taking the Jeep off-road?

Awesome—follow the dirt path up a ways.

Only one way to go.

What are we doing?

Ahh... as I said, first we're having a picnic.

And then?

We're gonna rappel down a two-hundred-foot cliff. And go fly fishing.

Hell yeah!

I told you it was going to be dangerous, didn't I?

True to my word.

Okay...this is it.

Park over there next to the picnic table.

Yes, this *is* private land.

I've been coming here for years.

Don't know how I did it. Just knocked on a door and asked.

Hard to refuse fly fishing charm I suppose.

So, let me get our stuff out and we can begin.

First, we eat …

Here's a sandwich, some chips and an orange.

Go to town.

Eh…???

You see, now that is *exactly* why I brought you here.

When you eat, you're all arrow and zero fletching.

All attention and zero awareness.

Give me that orange, Piglet.

Here's your first lesson in awareness.

Spiritual Badass Awareness Sight & Smell Exercise

Okay, my pink peccary piglet—we're going to start with a candle and then we'll get to the orange. Luckily, I brought a really nice lavender scented one. I'm going to guide you through the exercise right now. Afterwards, you should be able to do it at home with any pleasantly smelly object you choose.

(If you are at home, get a candle and find a comfortable quiet space where you won't be disturbed.)

Start with three deep breaths:

- Take a large inhale followed by a large exhale.
- Take another large inhale followed by a large exhale. One more time...
- Take another large inhale followed by a large exhale

Really, come on. Take those breaths. Don't skip.

Briefly tune in to the current state of your body: Is it tired, achy, hungry, relaxed, excited, hopeful, agitated, nervous, concerned or perhaps not feeling much of anything? Allow everything to be as it is. Just notice it.

Okay let's light the candle. (Please don't burn your house down.)

Take another deep breath:

- Place your attention on what the candle looks like.
- Notice its shape, color, movement, flickering flame, undulating smoke.
- Now notice...the act of...seeing the candle.
- While you are seeing the candle, notice you are aware that you are seeing it.
- Here's the really important part:
- Being *aware* that you are seeing the candle and not merely *seeing* it...is to recognize awareness.

- I will say it again: Being *aware* that you are seeing the candle and not merely seeing it...is to recognize awareness.
- Notice again that you are *aware* of seeing the candle.

Take another deep breath:

- Now...place your attention on what the candle smells like.
- Notice if it is strong, weak, harsh, flowery, sweet, pungent.
- Now notice… the act of...smelling the candle.
- While you are smelling the candle, notice you are *aware* that you are smelling it.
- Here's the really important part: Being aware that you are smelling the candle and not merely smelling it...is to recognize awareness.
- I will say it again: Being *aware* that you are smelling the candle and not merely smelling it...is to recognize awareness.
- Notice again that you are *aware* of smelling the candle.

Spiritual Badass Awareness Touch & Taste Exercise

Okay, now we can use that orange.

(If you are at home, get an orange or any piece of fruit and find a comfortable, quiet space where you won't be disturbed.)

Take a deep breath:

- Place the orange in your hand.
- Place your attention on what the orange feels like to the touch.
- Squeeze it slightly. Roll it between your palms. Rub it with a finger.
- Notice if it's rough, smooth, dry, wet, hot, cold, slippery, craggy...
- Now notice... the act of...touching the orange.
- While you are touching the orange, notice you are *aware* that you are touching it.
- Here's the really important part: Being *aware* that you are touching the orange and not merely touching it...is to recognize awareness.
- I will say it again: Being *aware* that you are touching the orange and not merely touching it...is to recognize awareness.
- Notice again that you are *aware* of touching the orange.

Take another deep breath:

- Now...take a piece of the orange (obviously you need to peel it first), place it in your mouth, and slowly begin to chew it.
- Place your attention on what the orange tastes like.
- Notice if it's sweet, sour, bland...
- Now notice... the act of...tasting the orange.
- While you are tasting the orange, notice you are *aware* that you are tasting it.
- Here's the really important part: Being *aware* that you are tasting the orange and not merely tasting it...is to recognize awareness.
- I will say it again: Being *aware* that you are tasting the orange and not merely tasting it...is to recognize awareness.

- Notice again that you are *aware* of tasting the orange.

Good job.

When I was in my twenties, I did all sorts of crazy things in the name of fulfilling my own particular existential yearning and lack. One of the things I tried was a sugar fast. For about four months, I tried to avoid all processed sugars. It was a bitch.

I was somewhat successful, but not entirely. I managed to avoid the usual suspects like cookies, candy, cake and ice cream—but that was about it. All sorts of products have hidden amounts of processed sugars: everything from cereal to canned corn...to, uh, raisins and peanut butter.

I ended up cheating badly—really badly—with a box of raisins and a jar of "natural" peanut butter. Cram enough of that sickly combo into your mouth and down your gullet and you'll get your sugar fix. I think I stuffed a whole box of raisins and about half a jar of peanut butter into my mouth one night. Vampires sucking the blood of newborn babies have more dignity than I did.

I'm not telling you this so you, too, can avoid the diabolical grip of glucose. I'm telling you this because this is how I became aware of the act of ...seeing, touching, smelling and tasting the orange, or in my case the boxcar of raisins and peanut butter.

In other words, evolution doesn't care, the universe doesn't care, and I don't care how you get the lesson—just as long as you get it:

Being aware that you are tasting the orange and not merely tasting it...is to recognize awareness.

It took a craven, crack cocaine, blood-induced, vampire dietary frenzy for me to realize how unaware I had been around seeing, touching, smelling and tasting. The sugar diet broke my unconsciously unaware pattern—and suddenly, I was aware of it all.

Did *awareness* cure me of my evil desire for sugar? Fuck no. I still desire sugar to this day, but I am also very aware of this desire… and when one is *aware* of a desire, an odd thing happens: The desire tends to loosen its grip. Now— *I'm in control because I'm aware.* Sugar is *my* bitch; *not* the other way around.

Being aware that you are tasting the orange and not merely tasting it...is to recognize awareness.

Being aware that you are driving the car and not merely driving it...is to recognize awareness.

Being aware that you are reading the book and not merely reading it...is to recognize awareness.

Being aware that you are seeing the sunset and not merely seeing it...is to recognize awareness.

Being aware that you are peeing in the toilet and not merely peeing...is to recognize awareness.

Being aware that you are watching TV and not merely watching it...is to recognize awareness.

Being aware that you are holding a loved one and not merely holding...is to recognize awareness.

Being aware that you are talking with your neighbor and not merely talking...is to recognize awareness.

Being aware that you are seeing and reading words and not merely seeing and reading...is to recognize awareness.

Being aware that you think and understand and not merely thinking and understanding...is to recognize awareness.

CHAPTER 11
IN THE ZONE

How to be in the zone-all the time-good or bad

A wareness doesn't give a fuck if you're having a good day or a bad day. Awareness doesn't give a fuck if you're happy or sad. Awareness doesn't give a fuck if you're lazy or productive. Awareness doesn't give a fuck if you're a good guy or a bad gal.

Awareness is just like Switzerland: World War Three and a zombie apocalypse could break out simultaneously, and Switzerland...would...not...give...a...fuck.

Okay. We'll circle back to the aforementioned idea in a minute...

What do Michael Jordan, Lebron James, Michael Phelps, Tiger Woods, Roger Federer and Lewis Hamilton all have in common? They are all masters at being in the zone. They are all masters of awareness.

The good news is that you don't need to be an NBA basketball star or a six-time- winning World Championship Grand Prix driver to gain access to awareness.

You can instead be a schmuck like me—aware, but no rock star; aware and a Dad; aware and a husband; aware and a good person; aware and doing the dishes; aware and working a 9-5 job; aware and in the zone for no particular reason.

You're done with lunch, right?

Good.

It's time to do dangerous shit.

Grab that bag and follow me.

Okay, awesome.

What you are looking down upon is the Rapidan river.

Those are class 2 rapids below us.

We're going to rappel down here...90 feet to be precise...take the canoe I have hidden down there, paddle downstream about half a mile and then fly fish.

Oh, man this is gonna be fun!

You're scared?

Ha!

You should be.

That's part of the lesson.

I want you out of your comfort zone.

I wanna show you that no matter where you are or what the circumstance— awareness is always available to you and awareness is always OKAY.

You'll be fine.

I've done this a thousand times.

I've got all the proper gear.

Here we go.

Spiritual Badass Awareness Hearing & Body Exercise

You walk up to the cliff edge in your rappel harness.

Your pulse quickens as you look far down to the bottom.

It's a looooong way down.

Your reptile brain screams, "Fuck, no!!!"

But your badass brain screams, "Fuck yes!"

Below you can hear the splashing, gurgling sound of the Rapidan River.

- Take a deep breath.
- Place your attention on the river sounds.
- Notice the gurgles, splashes, whooshes, waves, tones, pitch, depth, duration, etc.
- Now notice… the act of...hearing the river sounds.
- While you are hearing the river sounds, notice that you are aware you are hearing them.
- Here's the really important part: Being *aware* that you are hearing the river sounds and not merely hearing them...is to recognize awareness.
- Notice again that you are *aware* of the river sounds.

You are now in the zone of hearing awareness.

All is well.

Nothing to fear.

I hand you the rope, belay and carabiner.

You turn around and prepare to jump backwards down the cliff.

You see the other end of the rope safely rigged to the front Jeep winch.

Small pebbles crunch beneath your boots.

Slack is released

The rope tightens.

You take a deep breath.

You leap.

Your body flushes with adrenalin.

Your heart sinks with nervousness...and excitement.

You grip the belay-carabiner stop device and slow yourself.

Your legs land on the vertical rock wall in front of you.

All is okay.

You pause and look down.

All is well.

- Take a deep breath.
- Place your attention on bodily movement.
- Notice your muscles clenching, legs maneuvering, arms tightening, hands gripping, lungs breathing, pulse quickening.
- Now, notice the total act of body movement.
- While you are moving your body, notice that you are *aware* you are moving your body.

- Here's the really important part:
- Being aware that you are moving your body and not merely moving it...is to recognize awareness.
- Notice again that you are *aware* of moving your body.

You are now in the zone of bodily awareness.

Nothing to fear.

Awareness doesn't give a fuck about your fears.

Awareness is fine under all circumstances.

Awareness doesn't give a fuck about your excitement or nervousness or stress.

Awareness is fine, no matter what.

- Take a deep breath.
- Place your attention on bodily movement.

You leap again!

But this time, because you are totally and completely in the bodily aware zone—the leap is amazing!

It is fantastic!

Thrilling! Epic! Badass!!

You pause and then leap again, remembering to be bodily aware and present again.

And...

It's amazing all the way down!

You get better and better with each jump.

Finally you reach bottom, grinning from ear to ear.

You are in the spiritual badass awareness zone...

And nothing can fuck with you here.

I'm going to Star Wars this shit, too, 'cause I'm a total Star Wars nerd.

There's a scene in the first Star Wars movie, A New Hope, where Han Solo, Chewy and Luke Skywalker are all fighting Imperial TIE fighters from inside the Millennium Falcon. It's a grandiose space battle. Luke misses a few, but then gets better on the laser gunner and finally shoots down a few enemy ships. He whoops and hollers in excitement. Han immediately responds: "Don't get cocky kid!"

Truer words have yet to be uttered about the nature of the spiritual badass awareness zone.

I'm pretty damn good when it comes to getting in this zone, but learn from my experience...

This past summer Jeremy, my twelve year old son, two of my employees and I all went to the Universal Kings Dominion amusement park just north of Richmond, Virginia. Kings Dominion boasts The Intimidator 305—the 10th fastest roller coaster in the world. It drops you—you guessed it—305 feet at punishing 95 mile per hour speeds. This roller coaster scared the shit out of me. The first time I rode the thing I was a complete nervous wreck! I was NOT in the spiritual badass awareness zone. What I'm saying is this: "Don't get cocky kid!"

Awareness is pretty goddamned amazing and being in the awareness zone is even more amazing, but trust me—it will not turn you into a superhero. There will always be things—people, places, experiences, etc.—that scare you. And this is good: After all, you are a human from Earth and not a superman from Krypton.

At the end of our day at Kings Dominion, I rode The Intimidator 305 for a second time. I wasn't a 100% in the spiritual badass awareness zone but I did much better, and consequently, I enjoyed the shit buckets out of it.

Spiritual Badass Lesson:

Most badasses have a "zone" or several of them. Some of us are in the zone as we shred a mountain bike trail. Some of us are in the zone as we play chess. Some of us are in the zone as we program software. Some of us are in the zone as we masturbate in the shower (okay...well I'm not sure that qualifies as the kind of zone we're talking about here, but you get the idea...).

Find and identify *your* zone. The next time you're in it, try to remember to be aware of awareness. You'll be surprised at what you find....yep, you're already aware!

Use your experience in the zone as jumper cables for other experiences. You can be in the zone under more circumstances than you'd think.

CHAPTER 12
EMOTIONAL WRECK

How to be aware when
everything sucks

Over the years I've helped a lot of people through the badass spirituality process, both in person and online. If one thing is true and certain about this process, it's that everyone has emotional baggage. Sometimes that baggage is sitting right there on the shelf for the whole world to see, and other times it's hidden deep inside...not even available to the very person whom it's hiding in.

The further one drives down the spiritual badass road, another thing becomes true and certain: Sooner or later all that baggage, whether exposed or hidden, surfaces and has to be dealt with. As we noted in Chapter Six-Emotion / How to stop being an emotional iceberg, this process starts with attention. We start by placing our attention on emotions. And now, we continue by placing our *awareness* on emotions.

Now we'll concentrate on simply dealing with present tense emotions—both positive and negative. This is hard enough for most. We'll get to the old stinky hidden emotional baggage at another point in our journey together.

The short and skinny is this: Right now I'm gonna learn ya how to be more badass aware with your current arising emotions. How we do this has to be a surprise. If I prepared you and told you to get all emotionally worked up about this and that and the other thing, it would just be fake and BS; and as you may have surmised by now, I don't do fake and BS. Badass spirituality goes right for the jugular...

So—I am tickled you enjoyed our rappelling adventure.

Not so bad, right?

Some good news for when we head back: there's an easy hiking path we can take on our return to get to the Jeep at the cliff top.

Yes...we rappelled unnecessarily !

Okay, let's grab the canoe.

There should be a paddle and two life jackets.

...Check; it's all here.

Help me drag this thing to the river, will ya?

Thanks.

Cool. You figure out the life jacket?

Looks right.

Alright: paddle, life jackets, bag of fishing gear. Er...eh..I think we're all set.

You hop in front.

I'll steer and guide us from the rear.

What!? You've never been canoeing!?

You're kidding!

My friend, there will be many firsts today.

Okay—here we go.

I want you to know that no matter what happens, you are going to be perfectly fine.

Why the warning?

Because, friend…

I'm flipping the canoe…

Spiritual Badass Awareness Negative Emotion Exercise

Instantly you are tipped, flipped and thrown into the river.

Water immediately soaks your pants, shoes, shirt and undergarments.

The force of your weight submerges your head briefly beneath the surface.

The life jacket immediately pulls you up above the water.

Sideways in the water and in shock, you try to orient yourself.

Downstream!? Canoe? What's that? Paddle…?

What the fuck? Is it over my head!?

Where's the guide!?

You spin and now face upstream.

You hear someone shout "Feet first!"

You spin again, feet first downstream.

The waves swiftly carry you.

Just ahead you spot the flipped canoe. The guide, floating nearby, calls out

"You're fine! Just keep floating like that! You're almost through!"

Your heartrate pounds.

Adrenalin floods your body.

The waves smooth out and end.

You make your way to a small sandy shore.

You drag yourself to a bare spot, exhausted.

An emotional cocktail of fear, shock and anger courses through your brain and body.

- Take a deep breath.
- Place your attention on these negative emotions.
- Notice how they feel in complete detail: fear, shock, anger, shakiness, exhaustion, stress, bad, negative, dark, soaked, or uncomfortable.
- Now, notice the act of *feeling* these negative emotions.
- While you are feeling them, notice that you are *aware* you are feeling them.
- Here's the really important part:
- Being aware that you are feeling negative emotions and not merely feeling them is to recognize *awareness*.
- Notice again that you are aware of feeling these negative emotions.

You take a deep breath.

You are okay.

You realize: These emotions are perfectly justified and appropriate and actually not so bad.

You sit and wait for the guide to drag the canoe ashore.

The emotional cocktail of negative emotions evaporates faster than usual.

You watch as the guide heaves the canoe onto shore.

You calmly walk over to him …

And slap him in the face.

Most of us are on endless emotional roller coaster rides, bounced about by the twists and turns of life. Or—as you've just experienced, most of us are being dragged downstream as we kick and scream for safety and control. Our efforts to stop, block or prevent these emotions usually fall pathetically short. They return again and again and we are bounced around again and again. Often we are at war with emotions.

But you can't stop emotions. Badass spirituality is not about stifling or stopping any particular emotion or set of emotions. Badass spirituality is about finding the calm center in the middle of those chaotic emotions. *That calm center is awareness.*

When we stop to notice the act of being angry instead of just being plain old angry, something amazing happens. We invite awareness into the anger. The anger then softens…and it goes away quickly.

Badass spirituality is about inviting the space of awareness into *every* moment of our lives. When we deal with our emotions this way—with awareness as the emotions arise—our emotions usually don't fester into long-term hidden emotional baggage.

Oh, don't get me wrong...you have baggage. But, let's start with the small stuff. When you are good and ready, that baggage will surface naturally and you'll handle it like a pro kayaker in class five rapids.

Ouch—that was a good slap.

Yeah, I deserved it.

Sorry...but it worked, right?

I told you I'd go for the jugular.

I weighed the pros and cons. Pissing you off a little was worth the lesson.

Maybe you noticed..?

Negative emotions are powerful and can suck, but… negative emotions without awareness suck even more.

Awareness softened the bite, right?

And you bounced back quickly?

The neuroscientific term for this is called "emotional resiliency."

I'm okay if you're pissed off a little.

And now...I'm going to make it up to you.

No surprises this time.

We'll walk from here.

Follow me.

Spiritual Badass Lesson:

When the shit hits the fan, when you are stressed, when you are feeling like crap; when you're irritated, depressed, moody, angry, bitchy or grumpy—

Remember to do this:

Notice *awareness.*

Notice the act of being grumpy, angry, bitchy, moody, stressed or depressed.

And notice *awareness.*

No this won't miraculously fix all your problems.

Nor will it make you instantly feel good.

But it will give you some -----------------space.

When tightly bottled, stress and the gang (anxiety, anger, depression, grumpiness) are really stressful.

But stress and the gang—dumped into a big ole' spacious awareness canyon— dissipate quickly.

So...when stressed, remember to notice the act of being stressed. Noticing awareness creates ------------space, which reduces stress quicker.

CHAPTER 13
EMOTIONAL BLISS

*How to be aware when
everything is awesome*

So? You ready to catch a fish?

No. We don't eat the fish.

We practice catch and release; that's the credo of all great fly fishermen. Leave nothing—take nothing—except beautiful memories.

I've strung up the fly rod and put on a chartreuse Clouser minnow lure.

There's a fish I want to introduce to you.

He usually hangs out near a log around the next bend.

We can walk there.

When we get there I'll cast the lure, then I'll give you the rod. You strip the fly line and see if anyone's home.

Sound like a plan?

Awesome.

Let's catch you a beautiful memory.

Spiritual Badass Awareness Positive Emotion Exercise

Your guide motions to you, and you follow.

Slowly you begin walking downstream in the ankle-deep water along the shoreline.

Now that you're calm again, you notice just how silky and warm the water is.

And it's clear...gin clear!

Your guide motions to you to take a big breath.

You do so.

He then puts his index finger to his lips indicating a need for silence.

You slowly follow his lead, each foot sinking through the warm lush water onto the sandy river bottom.

You take in another big chest full of air.

You slowly round the bend and there—in all its blazing glory—is the setting sun, teetering on the horizon in bright cabernet sauvignon, rose and blood orange colors.

Its light glints and shimmers as it penetrates the emerald green mountain laurel lining the river bank. The light bounces and reflects off the river in a frenzied ballet of zigs and zags.

You notice the river gently meandering into the distance.

You hear its soft watery gurgle.

You hear the sounds of the evening birds twittering their last songs.

The scene is more than beautiful; it's bucolic...every atom filled with shimmering delight and charm.

Your guide motions *stop*.

You watch as he casts across the river and slightly down stream.

You see the log he mentioned earlier.

He hands you the rod and motions for you to strip.

You strip and..!!!!! Thwack-Pull-Pound-Whump!!!!

The rod bends in immediate response to a very large fish which has just attacked your chartreuse lure.

An emotional cocktail of wonder, excitement and joy overtakes your brain and body.

- Take a deep breath.
- Place your attention on these positive emotions.
- Notice the feelings in complete detail: nervousness, joy, happiness, delight, wonder, amazement, exuberance or surprise.
- Now, notice the act of *feeling* these positive emotions.
- While you are feeling these positive emotions, notice that you are aware you are feeling them.
- Here's the really important part:
- Being aware that you are feeling positive emotions and not merely feeling them is to recognize *awareness*.
- Notice again that you are aware of feeling these positive emotions.

You hear your guide scream "Keep stripping! Hold the rod tip up!"

You do as he requests.

The weight and force are immense...much more than you ever imagined.

How could a fish pull this hard?!

You slowly pull in the line, gripping the handle and reel with everything you've got.

Your forearm muscles burn.

The fish darts and dives powerfully.

Then—in one breathtaking moment the fish hurtles himself out of the water and cartwheels through the air in a spectacular display of might and determination.

That thing is huge!!

He drops back into the water. Your guide screams "He's still on!" Your heart pounds.

The fish pulls hard one last time.

And then, slowly...he runs out of steam.

His pull is weak now.

You can see the beast getting closer.

He is spent.

So are you.

Your guide stoops down and briefly pulls your prized fish out of the water; this was indeed an award-winning day of firsts.

First time rappelling.

First time canoeing.

First time falling out of a canoe.

First time catching a gorgeous, bronze and emerald green, five-pound Smallmouth Bass.

You think to yourself...

What a gloriously badass *and aware* day.

Another name for cultivating awareness amidst the ups and downs of our emotional lives is compassion. Compassion is a loaded word, much like the words "god," "love" or "enlightenment." It has acquired excessive baggage during its time of use in our lexicon. But if we strip it down to its bare bones, I think there is a place for it here in Badass Land.

So let's start with this: Yahoo!!! Your awareness of emotions qualifies you for a Master's Degree in compassion!! You have become compassionate! (Squirm. Ick. Fizzle. Pew.)

Yeah, I know. Exactly.

Like you, I didn't sign up for all this spiritual stuff to become "compassionate." I had no intentions of becoming the next Mother Theresa, Pope, Jungian Psychoanalyst or Yogi Sri Ram Doogle Dum of the third dynasty of Kashmir. I just wanted a little happiness, peace and sanity.

But— lo and behold, go figure, somewhere along the way I did indeed become "compassionate"...but only as required by the natural laws of the process, not by exaggerated social terms. In other words, I received grades just good enough to get my degree in compassion.

And so, if you continue to cultivate awareness during all your emotional ups and downs, you too will get your degree in compassion. Compassion just means--------space. You are simply creating an empty buffer--------- a space where your emotions are not judged, reacted to or dramatized. You just listen. You just see. You just accept. You are aware. Super simple.

There are two pretty cool side effects that usually come with the degree in becoming compassionate: One—you become more open, accepting and understanding of other people's emotions. Two—other people's emotions tend to drain you less. So yeah...in some instances, when the moon is waning on Tuesdays after 4:20 pm you appear to be Mother Theresa, Pope John Paul, and Yogi Badass-a-Das all rolled into one. (Yeah that was a cannabis reference. If you are clueless, Google 4:20.)

Why am I telling you this? Because I want to save you from all the anguish, guilt and pain that the word "compassion" has caused me over the years. Do not feel guilty, just because you are more aware or "spiritual," that you haven't magically transformed into a fucking saint. This is Spirituality for Badasses—not The Compassionate, All Positive, Do-Gooders Gratitude Guide to the Galaxy. (Gag me with a compassionate spoon.)

Spiritual Badass Lesson:

Be aware of positive emotions:

Being aware that you are enjoying the sunset and not merely enjoying it is to recognize awareness.

Being aware that you are liking that person and not merely liking him or her is to recognize awareness.

Being aware that you are loving your family and not merely loving them is to recognize awareness.

Being aware that you are laughing and not merely laughing is to recognize awareness.

Being aware that you are feeling good and not merely feeling good is to recognize awareness.

Being aware that you are feeling happy and not merely feeling happy is to recognize awareness.

Being aware that you are loving the taste of potato salad and steak and not merely loving the taste is to recognize awareness.

Being aware of your sexual enjoyment and not merely enjoying sex is to recognize awareness.

Un-hyped compassionate awareness:

You need not become an all compassionate bodhisattva saint yogi guru who saves the world. Saving yourself with a little awareness...a little compassion...is plenty.

CHAPTER 14
THINK AGAIN

*How to be aware of the constant
thoughts in your head*

A long time ago during the age of myth, a woman was sentenced to death by her village. It started with the voices in her head...

From a very early age, she could hear them coming and going at all times. Some of the voices were soft and welcoming. Others were harsh and judgmental. Sometimes they were helpful and other times they chattered away with no purpose.

One day she innocently mentioned the voices to her mother, but the scolding she received taught her never to mention them again. Years went by. The little girl transformed into a troubled teenager who could no longer keep the voices at bay. They seemed to bark at her every day all day long.

In desperation, she finally went to her family and fully confessed to having these voices in her head. Her family was shocked and saddened. They did what they could and called upon the village doctor. With great reluctance, the doctor visited the family and over the course of several weeks prescribed various herbs and potions. Nothing worked. The doctor finally recommended that the girl visit the village priest. The village priest, also with great reluctance, tried curing her with various incantations, prayers and meditations. But nothing he did helped her either.

The voices in the young woman's head continued. Exasperated, the priest sent her to the village elders. Having only the traditions of their village and tribe to follow, they did only what they could do...

pass her on to the gods. She was sentenced to death by watery funeral pyre. The girl sadly gave in to her fate and accepted their final judgement and "cure" for the voices in her head.

The villagers gathered down by the river and placed the girl, still alive, on the floating funeral pyre. They placed a large bundle of sticks and branches on top of her. Then tar was poured over the entire lot. The pyre was pulled far out into the river by a small skiff. On shore, a few words were spoken by the village elders. Then the archers were given the signal. Seven flaming arrows whizzed through the air. Three of them struck. The floating pyre immediately caught fire.

Shortly afterward, a large thunderbolt of lightning struck in the distance. The villagers scattered to find reprieve from the approaching thunderstorm, leaving the girl resigned to her fate. They had done all they could do for the cursed little girl with the voices in her head.

But fate was still to have its way with her. The thunderstorm and ensuing rain doused the funeral pyre before the fiery branches could reach her. The girl remained trapped at the bottom of the pyre, caught among the tarred branches. The thunderstorm created havoc on the river. The river waters rose; waves swirled and pounded and the pyre was violently rushed downstream, farther than any village resident had ever been before.

The girl awoke to several strangers surrounding her on a shoreline. She was taken to their village to convalesce. After several weeks of recovery, the girl was asked by the foreign village elders what had happened. The girl confessed all, including the detail about the voices in her head.

"Voice in your head?" exclaimed the queen village elder. "Why, those are just thoughts! You were just noticing your thoughts! Dear child, everyone in this village has voices in their heads! We are all aware of them. Welcome...Hera, is it? ...We have a lot to teach you."

Hera, of course, lived a long and prosperous life...eventually becoming the queen elder of the foreign village herself. And the voices in her head remained with her for the rest of her life.

After catching the fish of a lifetime, your guide gestures to follow him home.

You walk back along the shoreline, taking in the glorious color palette of the languishing sleepy sun. The birds have settled. The river is flowing. The earth is calm.

You plunge your feet though the water, delighting once again in the soft crunch of the sandy bottom.

You arrive at the beached canoe.

Both of you hop in.

You hear your guide say, "No tipping this time. Promise."

You smile...that event seems like yesterday now.

You hop in the front and your guide begins paddling slowly back upstream.

You take in the peaceful sounds of the river, and then you hear your guide exclaim loudly, "Pink Elephants!"

What the fuck! You think to yourself.

Your mellow now completely harshed, you glare at your guide.

He screams once more. "Five million dollar lottery winner!"

You glare once more at your guide and he yells yet again! "Aliens from Mars Attack!!!"

He then looks at you and says calmly,

"Thoughts, thoughts, thoughts. Think again my friend, and again and again and again...You can't stop them."

Spiritual Badass Awareness Thought Exercise

- Take a deep breath.
- Place your attention on these thoughts:
- *Pink Elephants! -Five million dollar lottery winner!-Aliens from Mars Attack!*
- Notice these thoughts in complete detail: the images they elicit, any feeling associated with them or any further ideas or thoughts produced from them.
- Now, notice the act of thinking thoughts.
- While you are thinking thoughts, notice that you are aware you are thinking them. Here's the really important part:
- Being aware that you are thinking thoughts and not merely thinking them is to recognize awareness.
- Notice again that you are aware of thinking thoughts.

Most people are married to their thoughts. And for most, the marriage is a bad one—an unholy alliance of oil and water, ups and downs, screaming and fighting and threats to walk out, leave or divorce. There's a constant codependent war of neediness and neurotic clinging at play with our thoughts. One minute they are our best friends and lovers; the next, they are Satan incarnate and the root of all evil. Our sickly love-affair/marriage with thoughts never seems to heal, change or get better.

So to this I say, "Fuck it. Get divorced."

I have found, both from personal experience and from helping others to deal with their thoughts, that divorce is the best and only solution.

Divorce your thoughts right now.

You can both still live in the same house. You can both take care of the kids. You can both have the same bank account. You can both even sit in your favorite chair every Friday night and drink shitty homemade margaritas while watching Breaking Bad and eating tacos. You can do all these things together forever until you're dead! But—thank god!—you'll no longer be fucking married.

In order to divorce your thoughts, all ya gotta do is insert awareness all the time, every time (no expensive lawyer required). Notice your thoughts. Notice the act of thinking your thoughts. Notice. Notice. Notice. Aware. Aware. Aware. Notice the constant stream of thinking thought BS that pours out of your brain. Do this until you create a space between you and your thoughts so large—so immense and so spacious—that no bridge will ever be able to span them again. No marriage will ever bind and trap them again.

Actually if you do this really well, you can't even call it a divorce. It's bigger than that. It's the separation of church and state! Irrevocable. Irreversible. Done forever. Constitutional.

I am being serious here...no exaggeration. Divorcing your thoughts is a very profound thing to do. (Don't confuse this with ending or killing or stopping your thoughts. I'm not saying that.

I'm saying divorcing…you ain't ever gonna get rid of or end your thoughts.)

I remember the day I divorced my thoughts: It was a heart pounding, can't un-see this shit, anxiety attack causing, existentially profound experience. I had been steadily gnawing away at the awareness bone until, one night at about 2 a.m., I woke up to a huge anxiety attack. I had reached rock bottom.

Every thought I had…had now finally been seen. And all of them were deemed to be—worthless turds. My identification and marriage with thoughts had ended.

This instant divorce caused an extreme anxiety attack. I thought I was going to die or, worse yet, go insane. My identity had changed, moved on and grown. I was not my thoughts. I was the thinker of the thoughts. I was the ONE aware of thoughts. I was the free space of awareness that contained the thoughts. The thoughts were just brain farts, lots of them, in a constant stream. Fuck thoughts.

Fuck those little turds.

The divorce was final and it stung a little, but the freedom ever since…ahh, to be single again!

Divorce your thoughts. You will not regret it.

How do you do it? : "Unicorns Puking Rainbows!"

Spiritual Badass Lesson:

Take a deep breath. Place your attention on this thought:

Unicorns Puking Rainbows!

Notice this thought in complete detail: the images it elicits, any feeling associated with it or any further ideas or thoughts produced from it. Now, notice the act of thinking this thought. While you are thinking this thought, notice that you are *aware* you are thinking it. *Being aware* that you are thinking this thought and not merely thinking it is to recognize awareness. Notice again that you are aware of thinking thoughts. Now, do the same with these thoughts:

- "Life sucks!"
- "I'm stressed!"
- "I hate my job!"
- "No one loves me!"
- "I hate that person!"
- "That person hates me!"
- "Why did he do that to me?"
- "What did I do to deserve that?"
- "Nothing goes my way!"
- "I'm unhappy..."
- "Fuck you!"
- "Fuck me!"
- "Really!?"
- "Oh, man!?"

Hey friend...

You doing okay?

Let's get this canoe back in its hiding place and then we'll zip up the path and get back to the Jeep.

We should have just enough light.

Follow me—the path starts here.

I hope you enjoyed our adventure together today.

I know I did.

You were awesome.

I hope I haven't scared you off.

...a few more feet.

There's the Jeep.

Give me a minute to pack the gear and undo the cable.

Okay.

You good driving back?

Awesome. Thanks.

Here're the keys.

Just head back the same way we came in.

So before I nod off while you're driving I want to extend an invitation:

You wanna join me on a cross country adventure? I have more crazy wisdom to share, teach and give if you're game. I dig your company. And well, why the fuck not, right!?

Your guide offers to extend the adventure across the country into god knows where, doing god knows what.

Holy shit!? you think to yourself.

Am I fucking crazy?

Am I really going to do this - with this crazy fuck?

As you drive, your guide nods off to sleep.

You ponder it some more.

Eventually you arrive at the answer.

Yes!

Yes!

Yes! I'm going to do this.

Why?

Because.

Because.

Because of the wonderful things he does!

Because I am a Badass! That's why!

You smile inside and think to yourself,

We're off to see the wizard...

END PART 2

Continue your adventure with J.:
Connect, share, laugh, grow & learn
with other books, articles,
videos, courses & more...

Go here:
www.spiritualityforbadasses.com

PART 3

The Ninja Warrior Jedi Mindfulness Trick

CHAPTER 15
MINDFULNESS IS A BEACH

*How to recognize the mindfulness
beach bitch when you see her*

You've probably seen the Mindfulness Beach Bitch. She's usually sitting crossed leg with her hands resting on her knees. She's wearing $116 Lululemon Athletica yoga leggings with a matching $58 coral striped tank top. Her fingers are formed into an exotic yogic Vulcan mudra thingy, indicating that she's a pro at this mindfulness serenity shit. She has long loosely flowing, perfectly conditioned, full, shiny and blonde hair. And the pièce de résistance? She is sitting on a tropical Caribbean beach devoid of all other human life, facing the beautiful cerulean blue waters while the sun sets on the horizon. Calm. Beautiful. Fucking perfect.

Don't be fooled for a minute. This bitch is Zen, all the way to the bank.

The Mindfulness Beach Bitch only exists on Madison Avenue in the shriveled up hearts and minds of advertising and marketing executives tasked with the sole, soul-less purpose of selling brand name, keyword searchable— mindfulness, yoga, meditation—clothing, goods, books, magazines and food to brand name people living in brand name neighborhoods across the brand name world.

I mean *Holy fuck power tool nuggets, Batman!* I have seen the Mindfulness Beach Bitch at the check-out counter at Lowe's! The Mindfulness Beach Bitch is the ubiquitous guilt-inducing, unattainable, you-can't-touch-this whore of everything dubious, disgusting and dastardly about the modern mindfulness movement. The Mindfulness Beach Bitch is evil.

That being said, get rid of the bitch and the beach; then...mindfulness..? Well, it's pretty fucking awesome.

Okay. Where to start?

First off, I am pleased as punch that you have decided to join me on what promises to be a most excellent adventure. We are going to make Bill, Ted, Harold, Kumar and Pee Wee all proud.

'Strange things are afoot at the Circle-K.'

You have no idea.

So...

Three weeks off from work—check.

Bag packed for hiking, biking, ballooning, rappelling, white water rafting, walking on coals, 48-hour Santeria Ayahuasca ceremony and a night spent in jail. Joking about most of these— maybe...

Clothing for when hot, cold, wet and dry—check.

Money for food, lodging and emergencies—check.

Blank journal to write strange shit down—check.

Phone and charger for obvious reasons—check.

Driver's license and keys to the Jeep—check.

Lenny the Iguana—Fuck!??

Lenny!? Where's Lenny?

Ohhhh...there you are!

This is Lenny...my little green pet iguana and soulmate.

I know. I know. I shouldn't be traveling with a reptile. Cruelty to animals and all that. Lenny's different. He likes cars. He's urban, hip and very tolerant. I have his snuggle spot, food and heater in the trailer if he needs it. And as you can see, there's a gnarled tree branch in the back seat, which Lenny loves. He's cool. Trust me.

Repeat after me: Lenny's a lovable lizard.

Now, rub his tummy for good luck.

Okay.

Direction?

Drive east, Kemosabe.

Why?

...'cause we're headed for the beach bitch of course!!

While you're driving, let me give you the real scoop about mindfulness:

I think we've established the fact that corporate mindfulness propaganda is now ubiquitous—from big box hardware stores to 7-11 to mindfulness porn sites where you can jerk off while getting your cosmic consciousness on. (Just kidding...I think.)

Mindfulness? What's the big deal?

In all seriousness...the big deal is neuroscience.

Neuroscience has proven that mindfulness is just plain good for you in the same black and white kind of way that science has also proven that smoking ten menthol-flavored Marlboros per day is, um...bad for you.

During the 1990s non-invasive medical technology, a fancy term for scanning and mapping the body or brain without cutting, drugging or leeching, blossomed and took off. FMRI, Pet Scan and EEG machines became more sophisticated and reliable, thus more widely used for peering into the mysteries of the human body.

It didn't take long before one particular scientist, Jon Kabat Zinn, had the bright idea of mapping and scanning the brain before and after several weeks of mindfulness exercises and training. Lo and behold, what he discovered was that this shit produced less stressed, calmer, and considerably more peaceful brains and bodies—and the proof was in the scans. The scans showed that mindfulness reduced physiological, emotional and mental stress across the board.

What this meant was that mindfulness could be used to treat anxiety, depression, addiction, anger management, physical pain, immune deficiency, cardiovascular problems, trauma rehabilitation, general stress, unhappiness and much, much more.

It didn't take long for the scientific community to embrace Jon Kabat Zinn's discoveries. And voila`! Here we are today with thousands of mindfulness centers and training programs throughout the world, including many located in colleges, universities and hospitals.

Thus— *everywhere we go* the Mindfulness Beach Bitch is watching our every move, hoping we'll throw some fat bucks her slutty way.

Okay.

Full stop.

Slam on the brakes.

Right here's good.

Oh shit! Sorry, Lenny!

Alright...well done.

Lenny forgives you.

Now, look me in the eyes.

Deep breath.

Here's what you really have to know about mindfulness:

You're going to learn a lot about attention, awareness and mindfulness—all necessary tools on your badass spiritual journey. But do not mistake these tools for the end-all-be-all. Awareness and mindfulness are to spirituality what masturbation is to sex … a great tool when you're not getting laid.

Our goal together is to get you laid. Trust me when I say that you are going to like getting laid—spiritually speaking of course. Awareness and mindfulness will seem like cheap old sex toys running on low-power D batteries when you experience getting spiritually laid.

Don't get me wrong. Mindfulness is awesome. On its own—it will make you "*10% Happier*," to quote news anchorman and mindfulness author Dan Harris. And in our current fucked up day and age, this ain't too bad, but…

But…I wanna do ya one solid better.

If you're gonna travel down this tricky, bumpy backassed road, you might as well go for the gold. Right? Is 100% happier all the time possible? Fuck, no. But 50% happier most of the time is definitely doable—and with that you'll have numerous peak getting spiritually laid 90% to 100% happier, pretty fucking awesome spiritual experiences and moments.

Not bad, right?

Oh, and you just might be wondering…all this talk about getting laid… *Who exactly will I be having sex with?*

Great question.

The answer:

You will be fucking the whole universe. (Now that's a badass answer and spiritual metaphor I guarantee you will NOT find on Oprah's Super Soul Sunday.) Okay, you can put it back in drive.

We're almost to the beach, bitch.

Mindfulness comes into full focus for an individual when repeated self-observation, attention and awareness—with complete ease and effortlessness— bring about a spacious, empty, clear and fundamentally okay internal presence, which has heretofore remained hidden, obscured or unnoticed.

Getting this mindful part to come into complete focus requires a little effort, practice and repetition. It's no different than going to the gym. You want mindfulness muscles and all the benefits that come with? You gotta lift some weight and pump some iron.

Imagine four layers, one on top of the other: Mind, Emotion, Body and Mindful Awareness. Most people live their entire lives with this layered order of magnitude arrangement: Mind out front hot and bothered, followed by the ups and downs of emotion, then the complications of the body and finally mindful awareness in fourth place, lost or buried in the chaos and confusion of the previous three.

Spiritual Badasses have equal access to and awareness of all four. None are higher or lower, better or worse than the others. And when all are equal, a degree of peaceful equanimity is achieved and purveys throughout. This equanimity is by no means perfect, but it results in a calm bay compared to the usual raging high seas of the person bereft of mindful awareness.

You continue to drive as your guide babbles on about this whole mindfulness thing.

You glance behind you quickly and notice something very odd.

Lenny! That ridiculous, but cute, green iguana residing in the back seat...

Holy God damn shit!

Am I seeing what I think I'm seeing?!

That fucking lizard is...mindful!

You watch as Lenny deliberately and methodically moves from one branch to another—each step slow, at ease and in perfect unified coordination.

Lenny is aware of his every step.

Lenny is completely comfortable in his little lizard body.

Lenny has no bullshit emotions hampering him.

Lenny is most definitely not bothered by any thoughts.

Lenny the Lizard...is a Ninja Warrior Jedi Mindfulness Master!

Brilliant.

You grin from ear to ear as you cross the bridge from mainland North Carolina into the Outer Banks National Wildlife Refuge and Seashore.

CHAPTER 16
GOOD TIMES BAD TIMES PT. 1

How to be mindful during a Led Zeppelin song played at high volume on the beach

In the days of my youth
I was told what it was to be a man
Now I've reached the age
I've tried to do all those things the best I can
No matter how I try
I find my way to do the same old jam
Good times, bad times
You know I had my share
When my woman left home
With a brown-eyed man
Well, I still don't seem to care
- Robert Plant

The trick of mindfulness is to find that part of you, during good times or bad, that doesn't seem to care.

Okay...slow down a bit.

Cool.

Turn left at that sign.

Yep, this is our camping spot.

...been camping at Cape Hatteras Frisco Campground for years now.

This will be the official classroom for your first mindfulness classes.

Good times, bad times!!

For your first class, I've arranged something pretty awesome.

Within a few minutes you find yourself on a high sandy dune bluff overlooking the vast steel blue Atlantic Ocean. The dunes spread out north and south as far as your eyes can see. You hear the powerful wash of the ocean against the shoreline—rhythmic, pulsating, and soothing.

After setting up camp your guide meanders off, phone in hand.

You settle down next to Lenny, who is happy as a bug in a rug in his large pop-up cage.

You watch as Lenny slowly, deliberately and—not fucking kidding—mindfully chews on some fresh cabbage.

He's happy.

You envy him.

Not a single thought in his poor little lizard brain.

Your guide returns. With a mischievous sparkle in his eyes, he motions for you to follow him.

He instructs you first, however, to get suited up for water and beach.

You do so, and within a few minutes you are following him down a weathered grey boardwalk which meanders across the low-lying swampy dunes.

He turns to you and says:

"Lenny!"

With that word you are oddly reminded of your own body, breathing, footsteps and gate.

You take a big breath.

You slow down.

Each step becomes a—fuck, a Lenny step!

Slow.

Deliberate.

Peaceful.

Delightful.

Really? I'm taking lessons from a reptile!?

You smile internally and keep on walking.

You reach the beach.

And there—before you—a magnificent, yet strange sight:

The roar of the waves against the *drenched* golden-brown sand is delightful, beautiful and mesmerizing…and…there, set up at the water's wavy edge is—

Are you shitting me?

—a massage table.

Your guide speaks:

"Like I said, welcome to the beach, bitch!"

He laughs.

Your guide motions for you to lie down. You look around, slightly embarrassed, but the sun is setting and there's no one around except an elderly couple hundreds of yards away.

You acquiesce.

Oh Lord, what have I gotten myself into?

"What you're about to experience is called a body scan.

"Close your eyes. Here's a pillow and a sheet if you'd like.

"You comfy?

"Welcome to Mindfulness Lesson 101."

The Basic Body Scan Exercise

"Take three deep breaths.

"Concentrate on the waves.

"Pay attention to the waves.

"Be aware of the waves.

"Be aware of awareness itself.

"Let everything be—just as it is—thoughts, emotions, body. Not trying to change anything. Just noticing."

You settle in and begin listening to the waves.

You listen to your guide…

"Place your attention and awareness on your toes."

You zero in on your toes, really noticing them: the sheet they touch; the remnants of sand between them; the damp feeling left over from the ocean. You wiggle them slightly.

"Place your attention and awareness on your feet and ankles."

You notice your feet: the slight soreness in your left ankle; the bottoms of your feet; the soles of your feet.

"Place your attention and awareness on your shins and calves."

You notice your shins: You remember the bike accident that left a scar that's still on your left shin when you were twelve. You notice your calves pressed against the table. Warm. A slight breeze undulating the sheet against them.

"Place your attention and awareness on your knees."

Your right knee itches but you soon let it go. Your left knee is void of any feeling. You notice the back of your knees slightly sweaty and touching the table.

"Place your attention and awareness on your thighs and upper legs."

You notice your thighs. Another itch on your left leg. You remember the mole on your right leg. You feel the sheet blowing again in the breeze against your legs.

"Place your attention and awareness on your groin, bottom and genitals."

You feel your buttocks pressed against the table. The sheet covers your genitals which are free of constriction due to the loose bathing suit you have on. You feel slightly embarrassed at the mention of your genitals. You allow this to pass and focus.

"Place your attention and awareness on your lower back, stomach and belly button."

You notice your stomach, still slightly full from the lunch you had a few hours ago. Your lower back is a little achy...probably from all the driving. Your belly button, an outie, is fine except...actually...crap! There's an itch on your belly button now. You wait. It passes.

"Place your attention and awareness on your upper back, chest and heart."

You notice your chest...the rising and falling of your diaphragm as your lungs breathe. You focus on your heart area. You notice its subtle beating. Your upper back, also slightly sweaty, is pressed against the table.

"Place your attention and awareness on your shoulders and neck."

You feel your shoulders, but your neck *screams* for attention.

Oh, right! It's been cramped since morning due to a bad pillow position or something.

You notice the slight cramp. You zero in on it. It subsides somewhat.

"Place your attention and awareness on your face, lips, nose, eyes and mouth."

You notice every inch of your face. You feel the slight heat and sweat on your nose. Your eyes are slightly tired from the sun and sea and sand. Your mouth is slightly parched, but okay.

"Place your attention and awareness on your forehead, scalp, ears and hair."

You notice your forehead, remembering a slight lingering headache you had this morning. Your scalp and hair are hot from the sun. Your ears are slightly warm but comfortable.

"Take a deep breath. Now place your attention and awareness on the whole of your body. Quickly scan it from head to toe.

"Notice the act of noticing.

"Notice an empty, clear internal presence which is doing the noticing.

"Notice this internal presence is always there and always okay.

"Good job.

"Rest for a bit."

You continue to relax, allowing the beach body scan to do its work. You are alert and at peace.

And then...

From out of nowhere ...

A portable mp3 player blares Led Zeppelin's *Good Times, Bad Times* ...at a very high volume.

Spiritual Badass Lesson:

Mindfulness at the beach is easy and it's an advertising executive's wet dream. Everyone could be a mindful master if we all learned at the beach. But for most of us, reality isn't the beach; it's concrete and traffic jams and iPhones and emails and deadlines.

But you gotta start somewhere and there ain't nothin' wrong with the beach...bitch. Just as long as you see her for what she is.

The body scan exercise is vitally important on the road to badass spirituality and there are a million versions of it. Anything that draws attention and awareness into the present moment, into noticing the body, into accepting all the thoughts and emotions that arise in the body and into noticing mindful awareness itself...is badass, okay and recommended.

And, if all else fails...get an iguana.

CHAPTER 17
GOOD TIMES BAD TIMES PT. 2

How to be mindful when floating ocean beasties sting like shit

O kay...that was too easy.

"It's time for Mindfulness Lesson 102.

"The sun is setting.

"I'm hoping I timed this right.

"But we'll see.

"Follow me."

After breaking down the massage table, your guide plods off down the beach and motions you to follow.

You do so...in a very relaxed state.

Lenny is the shit! you think.

This mindfulness stuff is da bomb.

Your guide rounds a small beach bluff and then peers out into the ocean.

He motions for you to follow as he jumps headfirst into the surf.

You jump in after him.

The salty cool ocean water embraces your whole body.

The powerful surf jerks you around until you swim out beyond the crashing waves.

In deeper now, you wait—treading water and wondering what your guide is up to.

He has a slight look of apology on his face...

And then...

"Christ Almighty! What the fuck!" you scream.

A very painful stinging sensation registers on your right lower calf, and then you see the culprit: a grapefruit-sized jellyfish floating a foot away in the water. It has just stung you.

The pain is piercing.

"God fucking damnit!"

You scream again and then swim onto shore as fast as possible.

"Shhhiiiiit!"

A less severe sting—right upper chest now.

And now you see what you hadn't seen before...

There are jellyfish *everywhere.*

Your guide stumbles onto shore.

You notice for the first time that he has his shirt on. It's long sleeved.

Fucker. You think to yourself.

152

Your guide walks up to you.

"Let me see. Hmmm...not too bad. Just two."

"Trust me, in five minutes it will pass."

What the fuck were you think—?

"Lie down on the sand."

The Pain Body Scan Exercise

"Okay—Take three deep breaths. This is Mindfulness Lesson 102."

You do so angrily and reluctantly.

"Ohhhh...it stings like shit!!!"

"Breathe...

"Place your complete attention and your awareness on the stinging."

As best as you can, you place your awareness on the stinging. The exact center of the pain. The pulsing, the bite, the heat coursing throughout your leg and upper chest.

"Notice everything about it..."

You notice all there is and *more* about the sting: the pain, your leg, your reactions, your thoughts, your emotions and suddenly—

Fuck me...holy shit—Lenny!

Awareness.

There's awareness—calm, cool, collected—even during this sting!

Holy shit! There's awareness even during the pain!

There's awareness!

The pain subsides ever so slightly. For a nanosecond, you completely forget it during your awareness epiphany.

"Breath into the pain. Feel it. Allow it. Stop fighting it."

You do so—and the pain subsides even more.

Awareness again.

There it is!

Silent, clear, empty...

Fucking weird...

The pain slowly lessens to a tolerable level.

Holy crap, that stung but...

"So, did it work?"

"Yeah...it worked, asshole!" you reply.

Your guide nods his head.

"Sorry, friend. Mindfulness is worthless unless you discover it under inhospitable circumstances. Those were common sea nettle jellyfish; they hurt like hell, but they aren't lethal...well, usually."

Usually? Are you fucking kidding me?

You steam with anger again and then catch yourself:

Wait a minute? Even now...during my anger? Awareness...shit!

What   is   this?   Who   am   I?   What   the   fuck?

"Okay cowpoke, time to get back.

"Get up.

"I know. I'm an asshole.

"...never promised this would be lollipops and unicorns.

"I do promise, however, by the time this is over you'll have the heart of a frog and the skin of an alligator."

"Oh, right—you don't know that story, do you?

"Lenny told it to me.

"Listen up now.

"I'll share it with you as we walk back to camp."

Still slightly perturbed, but physically okay, you listen while your guide walks and talks.

With the stinging dissipated, you walk...your wounded pride bothering you more than the two lingering red stings.

Did he just say that his iguana told him this story?

Huh?

Down in the Dismal Swamps of the Louisiana Bayou, there lived a frog and an alligator. The frog's name was Tuna and the gator's name was Butch. It don't take much imagination to reckon the temperament of these two animal types. Tuna was a fair, giving, sensitive type and Butch was an old, mean cantankerous type. I guess you could say that the frog was thin-skinned and the gator was thick-skinned.

Tuna and Butch didn't have nothin' much to do with each other, 'cause they lived in opposite sides of the swamp. As a matter of fact, most of the frogs in this section of the Bayou lived in Frogtown (as they called it) and most of the gators lived in Gatorville (as *they* called it).

It was an equitable arrangement, but it suffered from one major flaw:

Once a season, the local human types swept through both Frogtown and Gatorville huntin' everything. The frogs were captured, killed, eaten and used by frog hunters and the gators were captured, killed, eaten and used by gator hunters. It sucked. For about a month each year, Frogtown and Gatorville turned into a pandemonium-laced death trap. That is...until one fateful mid-season day.

Tuna happened to be hoppin' about just outside Frogtown and Butch happened to be lazin' about just outside Gatorville. Something scared Tuna out of his wits and he jumped a good six full feet into the air and landed—where do ya think? Yes, sir...right on Butch's back.

Now, sumpin' interesting I ain't told ya about Tuna was this: His kind secreted a nasty smellin' and slightly toxic venom when scared. So when Tuna landed on Butch's back, he let out a nasty bunch of the stuff and slimed Butch real good. Butch's swampy thick gator skin just made the slimy venom worse. And here's when things got interesting. The thing that had scared poor Tuna was, in fact, one of the human-type frog hunters. Just after Tuna landed on Butch's back and splattered him with toxic goo, the human type came splashin' through the reeds. But when the human type saw Butch, he just about soiled his pants and ran off. The next day, to add serendipity to synchronicity, a gator hunter got the jump on Butch but when he took one whiff of him, he also ran off.

Now Tuna and Butch weren't the smartest animal types in the swamp, but they recognized a good thing when they saw it. A few days after the fateful incident, Tuna sought out Butch and proposed a plan. It was genius: Half of Frogtown moved over to Gatorville and half of Gatorville moved over to Frogtown. And whaddya' think happened? From then on out, not a single frog or gator hunter ever bothered none of them again. The thin-skinned frogs were protected by the gators and the thick- skinned gators were protected by the frogs.

So, what's the moral of this story? Well...first of all, don't go fuckin' around with any of them frogs or gators down in the Dismal Swamp of the Louisiana Bayou—especially if they're named Tuna or Butch. And second of all...it's best to have both thin skin and thick skin.

Spiritual Badass Lesson:

Mindfulness has an odd by-product: It will make you both thin- and thick-skinned. Paradoxically, you will become both more open, aware, sensitive and compassionate *and* more confident, centered, strong and decisive.

Mindfulness is the ability to be both the frog and the alligator. When you can recognize that part of you which is always okay, clear and free during both good times and bad times, you will have become a mindfulness master...

...just like Lenny.

Your guide takes you back to camp. Once there, the rest of the evening passes without drama, thankfully. The camp site is spacious and the grilled fish on the open barbeque tastes divine. Lenny chomps away mindfully again...the little fucker...on a cuisine of spinach leaves and carrots, with a whole organic strawberry for dessert.

That lizard eats better than we do, you think.

You are slightly relieved to hear that tomorrow is a rest day...just ocean, beach, and sun. Yahoo!

You sleep soundly, lulled by the monotonous rhythm of the distant crashing waves.

The next day passes as planned. While lying on the beach, you ponder the very strange encounter with mindful awareness...

or yourself or...is that what you'd call it?

This open spacious presence?

… Me?

And you catch it again…

Who or what is asking that question?

At about five in the afternoon your guide walks up to you and announces, "Okay beach bum, pack your things. Let's get dressed; tonight we're going out on the town! You and me and Lenny are going to Lucky's Two Stroke Biker Bar!"

You pause, then groan and slowly get up from your comfy beach spot and follow the guide.

Oh shit, a biker bar!? And Lenny? Really? Oh God, what is he up to?

How to be mindful when drinking tequila shots & more ...

Lucky's Two Stroke Biker Bar is exactly as it sounds. It's an old mostly wooden shack with a neon sign out front sized just right for air traffic control.

Out back, you can see a long, dilapidated pier stretching out into the relatively calm, flat Pamlico Sound. You can hear the thump-thump-thump of a kick drum and some muddled rock music of a band coming from somewhere inside.

The parking lot is vast and filled with motorcycles, trucks and an assortment of muscle cars.

Not a Prius in sight.

You pull up in the Jeep and find a place to park.

Very carefully, you back in between two rows of very black, very chrome and very intimidating mostly Harley Davidson motorcycles.

Please God, let me back in straight.

Mission accomplished, your guide hops out and gently wraps Lenny around his neck and shoulders.

Am I seeing things or does the lizard look excited to be here?

"Lenny is super excited to be here."

Did he just read my mind?

"This...is going to be epic."

I am fearing those words.

"Come on—follow me."

"Okay."

Now...before we get all debauch, degenerate and delinquent here (I like alliteration and triple synonyms.), we should probably have a talk about my stance...Spirituality for Badasses stance...on alcohol, drugs and substance use and abuse. It bears mentioning, so right brain—calm down and relax; left brain—listen up.

I've met all sorts of spiritual types who have all sorts of opinions about drugs and alcohol. Let's take marijuana for example: Some believe the stinky sticky weed is a gift from the gods that promotes enlightenment, heavenly visions and encounters with the wee-green people of the southern hills. Others think that Satan himself cultivated the green beast to trick all humans into a life of drug addiction and criminal servitude.

Personally, I think pot is just an easy way of saying, "Fuck this shit, I'm checking out for a while." There ain't nothin' grandiose or diabolical about it....sorta like ascribing mystical visions to a can of Budweiser. It's just fuckin' pot.

I feel pretty much the same way about alcohol: If used in moderation, with intelligence and awareness...no harm done.

But of course, I am perfectly cognizant of the fact that quite a few people who may be interested in a book called Spirituality for Badasses may also have a less than healthy relationship with drugs and alcohol. To those, I'd point to this single salient paradox: Spiritual growth doesn't easily happen when you're addicted or prone to abusing drugs or alcohol or are in denial about it. *But* if you are addicted and can rise above the denial, you are in a most beautiful and exquisite place for spiritual growth to begin. Why is this? Simple…it's because you are in pain, and the universe knows it.

I don't know how to explain this, but the universe can hear your pain loud and clear. It can feel your pain intimately. It can see your pain. It can smell your pain. It can taste your pain. And your pain is the most beautiful song the universe has ever heard. It is your heart shouting. So, anybody who tells you that you are bad, or evil, or somehow inferior because of your addiction or pain—well, they can go fuck themselves on the street corner across from Wendy's.

Addiction and pain are invitations to wake up to something pretty damn cool...the very universe itself. The funny thing is that the universe is already within you—you just don't realize it or see it that way. But we're here to help change that. That's what this badass spiritual adventure is all about.

Look, man...I mean, I haven't exactly reinvented the wheel here, right? There's this eighty-three-year old organization with over 2 million members: It's called Alcoholics Anonymous. AA rocks because it offers a broad spiritual solution to a very specific problem and it does so in a very open, sensible and nondogmatic fashion.

So, yeah. Before we go into Lucky's Two Stroke Biker Bar to get hammered in a very wild, weird and mindful way—you gotta ask yourself this: Is my drinking or drug use just for the occasional fun or relief, or is it masking and numbing a deeper pain that I am in denial about? You know the difference.

Your guide marches you up to the old creaky wooden doors of Lucky's Two Stroke Biker Bar. Before entering, he looks you in the eyes and deadpans:

"You will never find a more wretched hive of scum and villainy."

You chime in while laughing:

"Yes, yes...I know; we Star Wars nerds must be cautious."

You walk in and behold...the Star Wars Mos Eisley Cantina and Tavern is, in fact, a real place.

You are immediately drenched in a cacophony of sight, sound and smell.

Black leather. Ponytails. Neon signs.

Crowded bar. Chrome stools. Loud band.

Scantily dressed waitress. Golden-hued cheap beer.

Cigarettes. Was that a whiff of pot?

Pool table. Crosses. Skulls. Motorcycle Club symbols.

Lettering you can't read.

And what's...that? a..? Yes, a boa constrictor!

And there's a parrot on that guy's shoulder!

Is that a..? It is! Another iguana!

Your guide yells "Follow me—let's sit over there."

You walk up to the bar with him and miraculously two bar stools open up. You grab them. Your guide smiles.

"This is Lenny's favorite bar!"

"I completely understand!"

The bartender, a No BS-looking stocky woman in her late fifties, is serving drinks at the far end of the bar. Your guide waves his hand and, within a minute, she rolls over.

Upon arrival, she spots the iguana on your guide's shoulder. She smiles and proclaims, "I see you and Lenny are back for more! What'll it be tonight, guys?"

Before you can say anything, your guide blurts out, "Two beers and four shots of tequila, please."

"Tab?" she asks.

"Yes," your guide replies.

Oh fuck, I'm in trouble, you think.

The bartender meanders a few feet away to get your drinks.

"That was lucky," your guide says.

"What was lucky...the bar stools?"

"No—that was Lucky, the bartender. She's the owner!"

"Oh!" you laugh, and then look nervously as she returns with enough alcohol to make a rhinoceros pass out.

"Thanks, Lucky!" your guide says.

She gives him two thumbs up and then walks away to tend to another customer.

Your guide looks at you and asks, "Okay—you ready for Mindfulness Lesson 301?"

"No...I am not," you reply.

"Good. You're gonna love this. Trust me!"

The Inebriated Body Scan Exercise

"Let's begin...take three deep breaths."

You take three deep breaths, and because you are slightly nervous and somewhat overwhelmed, doing so immediately relaxes you.

"Allow it all in—the sights, sounds, smells.

"Pay attention to everything going on in the bar.

"Be aware of everything happening in the bar.

"Be aware of awareness itself.

"Let everything be in you—just as it is—thoughts, emotions, body. Don't try to change anything. Just notice."

You allow the ambience of the bar in.

"Cheers, friend. Now have a shot."

Your guide slides one of the shot glasses filled with clear tequila toward you.

Here we go.

You down the shot of tequila. Its sweet, prickly taste burns your mouth and throat slightly. You immediately feel its warmth settle into the bottom of your stomach.

"Place your attention and awareness on your toes."

You zero in on your toes, noticing them as they dangle in your leather shoes below the lower steel foot rail under the bar. You pull them up and rest them on the rail. As you move your feet, you really notice the alcohol. Your legs, feet and toes are getting comfy and warm.

"Place your attention and awareness on your feet and ankles."

You notice your feet, the bottoms of your feet, the soles of your feet and your ankles. You can't help but notice the effects of tequila now. Your toes, feet and ankles are super comfortable.

"So, you're probably noticing the slight effects of the tequila by now. Stay with it. Allow it. Be aware of it. Notice awareness itself. Place your attention and awareness on your shins and calves."

You notice your shins and calves. And then—bang! Awareness shifts into focus.

Clear, open, empty spaciousness.

Presence. Am I this? Yes!

This is me!

"Take another shot and then place your attention and awareness on your knees and legs."

You down another shot, without hesitation this time. The newly focused awareness is on fire now.

167

The alcohol immediately fills you with the same warmth and tingling. It doesn't take long for the effects of the second shot to take hold.

You remember your knees and legs. All are feeling warm, wobbly, good and fun right now.

Then, again—

Aware! Conscious! Clear!

The awareness witnessing presence peers through the inebriation and dominates it. And you realize...

The body is drunk, but I am not!

You say it aloud so your guide can hear:

"I'm drunk, but—I am not drunk!"

"Exactly!" he replies. "Now take another shot and place your attention and awareness on your groin, bottom and genitals."

You down the third shot of tequila.

Oh boy, I'm gonna be fucked up. But who or what is I? Yes, absolutely! The conscious, aware me is not drunk!

You place your attention and awareness on your bottom, genitals and groin. You notice that the more attentive and aware you become, the further you are extricated from the drunk body.

The real me never moves or budges an inch!

Your guide yells out, "Keep going! Now place your attention and awareness on your back, stomach and chest."

You notice your lower back, stomach and chest region—all through the side effects of the alcohol.

You blurt out, *"So this is the lesson?! I'm drunk...but awareness is not!?"*

"Yes!!" your guide replies. "One more to go!! Take the last shot!"

You do so, downing the tequila in one gulp.

"Place your attention and awareness on your shoulders, neck, face and head."

Your body becomes a swirling cyclone of inebriated conscious awareness. You've never been this drunk before or *this kind of drunk* before. The paradox of utter intoxication mixed with conscious attention and awareness is truly strange.

"I'm shitfaced!" you proclaim to your guide as you grab the nearby mug of beer and take a gulp.

"Yes, indeed you are," your guide replies.

He continues. "But who are you really?! I think the one who is not shitfaced, the one who is okay, who is clear, who is always present—that one. That one can hear me loud and clear right now."

You look at your guide and reply.

"Yes...that part...hears you."

So, fucking odd.

"Lenny!"

Right at that moment, you watch in bemused drunken astonishment as Lenny leaps from your guide's shoulders across a waitress' tray of dirty plates and onto the shoulder of a very large biker. You see why Lenny did it. On the biker's shoulder is the iguana you spotted earlier.

The surprise of Lenny's jump is just enough to make the big biker lose his footing and topple over onto the table of four other bikers. Lenny quickly scrambles away and your guide scoops him up.

But the damage is done—and in a place like this, it doesn't take long for the fists to start flying. One fist is thrown, then another and another. You laugh uncontrollably at the bedlam unfolding around you—and then...everything goes black.

Spiritual Badass Lesson:

I'm not advocating that everyone needs to go to a biker bar and get shitfaced, but I am advocating the need to discover mindful awareness under multiple circumstances.

Most of us don't live under rocks. Therefore, Spiritual Badass Mindfulness tricks need to work out in the world—not just in the comfy setting of your bedroom, meditation spot or cushy Costa Rican spiritual retreat center with silk sheets and organic breakfasts, lunches and dinners. You get the idea.

This shit takes practice. Drawing out mindful awareness is both an art and a science. The science dictates repetition, practice and patience. The art asks for boldness, courage and a little bit of craziness. Cheers.

CHAPTER 19
OH FUCK WHAT HAVE I DONE?

How to be mindful during a crisis

You open your eyes. Drool is dripping from the corner of your mouth down the side of your cheek onto the cold steel bench you are lying on.

…The same bench you were thrown on at 2 a.m. last night…by the police.

…The same bench you passed out on…in the holding cell.

Oh, fuck! What have I done?

You pop up, wincing as your brain protests with a pulsing headache. You see a dozen other biker-looking characters standing, sitting and lying around. The cell is standard issue white concrete, gun metal steel barred doors and fluorescent lighting. And then you notice…

Something is not quite right.

Why…why can't I see?

You touch your left eye and realize it's swollen shut.

Oh shit.

"Yeah, um…it looks how it probably feels."

Your guide is sitting next to you on the far edge of the bench.

"Let me take a closer look…

173

"Well, the bad news is your eye is swollen shut; the good news is we're getting out soon and going to the emergency room."

You try to respond verbally but all that snorts out is a muffled grunt.

"That was one hell of a punch you took last night. I thought we'd be able to escape, but I couldn't exactly move you with you being knocked out on the bar floor and all. Then the police showed up...and, well, you see what happened next."

"Where's Lenny?" You manage to grumble.

"They've got him in a cat-carrying box in the other room. Can you imagine the indignity!? A cat box! He'll be more pissed than you are now, I suppose."

Fuuuuuuuck.

You then lie back down on the bench and close your one good eye.

You wake up again...this time propped up on a hospital bed. There's a nurse fiddling with some machine in the far corner and your guide is seated on a generic looking green and yellow chair next to your bed. From the streaks of light shooting out from behind a long blue curtain, you surmise that it's sometime in the morning.

"Ah...back again, I see".

"Where are we? How'd..."

"You passed out—or, eh...fell asleep again. We're at *The Outer Banks Hospital*. Your eye's going to be fine. The swelling has

174

already gone down. But...glad we're here. Just a precaution." The nurse smiles at you and then adjusts your bed.

"Drink this," she says.

"Is this for my eye?"

"No" she replies. "It's vitamin water for your hangover. Eat this banana also. High in potassium."

She hands you a banana. You take it and begin peeling, then eating it.

"Okay, I'll release you in about an hour. You're fine. Stay outta biker bars for a while, will ya? I've got two more of you idiots down the hall."

"Yes, Ma'am," you reply.

She walks out of the room. Your guide looks at you as she exits and blurts out, "She's no fun."

"You're a menace," you reply.

"Guilty as charged! Whaddya say we take advantage of this situation and get another mindfulness lesson in?"

You grunt.

"I'll take that as a yes."

"Well, okay—before we start, let's take a look at the facts. Number One: you're in a hospital bed recovering from a black eye and a pretty harsh hangover. Number Two: you have been charged—along with myself and a dozen other goofballs, I might add—with disorderly conduct in a public place and you now have a misdemeanor record in the state of North Carolina. Number Three: you paid a $500 fine for this privilege. Number

Four: your little soiree here in Doctor Land is probably going to cost you another $200 to $300...that is, unless you have a low enough deductible on your health insurance. Number Five and last but not least: Your immediate family was notified by both the police and the hospital about all these shenanigans. I think that about sums it up. How do you feel?"

You look up, take a breath and open your mouth to speak.

"Don't answer that. I know this seems like a crisis and on the exterior, it is, in the grand scheme of things, yes...but a small one. Inside, though, trust me; it's a nothing burger. Let me prove it to you."

You give your guide a look of disgusted acceptance. "Breathe deep...three times."

You take three deep slow breaths.

"Let's zero in on what's happening right now. First, place your attention and awareness on your thoughts. What's going on there?"

You take a minute to think about your current thoughts and reply.

"Um...my thoughts are everywhere, like a rat racing around in a maze with no escape—agitated, relentless, nonstop, nervous, I guess. I keep trying to come up with a solution to this catastrophe that'll make it go away...but can't."

"Good. Emotions?"

"I'm angry, stressed. I feel untethered. Everything is out of my control. Anxiety through the roof."

"Good. And what is your body doing?"

"Body is clenched, nervous, tender...wounded."

"Okay. Great. Excellent. So, let's go find the part that is free and clear during all this—okay?"

You nod positively.

"We're going to do another body scan; except this time, we're going to add everything you just described to me. We'll call it the feeling state of crisis. Got it?"

You nod.

The Feeling State of Crisis Body Scan Exercise

"Breathe in and out...deeply.

"Again breathe...and one final time.

"Now, recall everything you just described to me about your current feeling state—thoughts, emotions and body. I'd like you to simply allow this feeling state to be with you at a 100% level. We're not trying to change it; not trying to make it better or go away. Quite the opposite, in fact. We want to invite ALL of it in."

You do the best you can, inviting the whole thing in.

"Place your attention and awareness on this total feeling state of crisis. Invite it to be here completely."

Alright, already. Shit, I am agitated! Let it in.

You listen to your guide...

"Place your attention and awareness on your toes."

You zero in on your toes, noticing them; the sheet they are beneath; the viewing angle you have of them from your hospital bed. You wiggle them slightly.

"Place your attention and awareness on your feet and ankles."

You notice your feet, the insteps, the soles of your feet, and your ankles.

"Now—once again, place your attention and awareness on the total feeling state of crisis. Invite it to be here completely."

You breathe in and think to yourself...*agitated, relentless, nonstop, nervous, angry, stressed, untethered, clenched, tender, wounded.*

"Notice awareness. Notice what is aware. Notice how it is untouched, clear and free."

You are jolted by the interruption. *Awareness? Okay—okay— wow, true...it is untouched—even during this.*

"Breathe. Place your attention and awareness on your shins and calves."

You notice your shins. You notice your calves pressed against the hospital bed.

"Place your attention and awareness on your knees."

You notice your knees. *Both are achy. Oh, right...bruised from the fall in the bar. What a fucking mess! Ugh, more thoughts...*

"Once again, place your attention and awareness on the total feeling state of crisis. Invite it to be here completely."

You pause and again think to yourself...*agitated, relentless, nonstop, nervous, angry, stressed, untethered, clenched, tender, wounded. But awareness...is...okay!?*

"Notice awareness. Notice what is aware. Notice how it is untouched, clear and free."

I get it. I get it. Shit. I really do.

"Place your attention and awareness on your thighs and upper legs."

You notice your thighs. *Itch on my right leg...*

"Place your attention and awareness on your groin, bottom and genitals."

You feel your buttocks and lower back on the angled hospital bed. Your genitals are free due to the hospital gown you're wearing. *Thank God I'm under this sheet. Thoughts. Thoughts. Thoughts. Thoughts about thoughts...*

"Place your attention and awareness on your lower back, stomach and belly button."

You notice your stomach, still clenched and tight from stress. *Hey, did it just unclench a little? Yeah, I think it did. And that, wow! That makes my lower back feel better. Okay...okay...*

"Again, place your attention and awareness on the total feeling state of crisis. Invite it to be here completely."

Agitated, relentless, nonstop, nervous, angry, stressed, untethered, clenched, tender, wounded. But, but...not so much anymore. Awareness—clear, empty. Nothing...

"Notice awareness. Notice what is aware. Notice how it is untouched, clear and free."

Yes! Inside the crisis is nothing.

"Place your attention and awareness on your upper back, chest and heart."

You notice your chest—the rising and falling of your lungs as they breathe. You notice your heart area. *Still a little on edge, tight, anxious. That helps...emptiness, nothingness—always there. Weird. Weird. Weird. Better...*

"Place your attention and awareness on your shoulders and neck."

Shoulders ache also. Maybe the fall...

"Place your attention and awareness on your face, lips, nose, eyes and mouth."

Oh God, my eye! Was worried about blindness. Ridiculous. All okay. Stress. Stress. Stress. Face okay. Awareness... free ...wow. Inside the crisis—nothing burger.

"Place your attention and awareness on your forehead, scalp, ears and hair."

Lingering hangover headache. But better now.

"Take a deep breath. Now place your attention and awareness on your whole body. Quickly scan it from head to toe."

"Notice the act of noticing."

"Notice that empty, clear, internal presence which is doing the noticing."

"Notice that this internal presence is always there, always free and always okay."

"Even during a crisis."

Yes—noticing—free—even...during a crisis.

Nothing burger...

"Rest a bit more. I think we can leave soon. I'm going to go get the Jeep. Meet you at the front desk?"

"Okay, cool." Aware of saying "Okay, cool." Aware of it all. Aware that yes, really, I am okay and...cool.

As your guide exits, you sit up and then hop off the hospital bed. You walk over to the window with the drawn blue curtains. You open them wide. A flood of sunshine smacks you in the face, causing you to squint. You close your eyes and take a long deep breath.

Damn, that feels good.

Spiritual Badass Lesson:

Crisis comes in two forms:

When we are born, we immediately begin the existential crisis of life and death. Most human beings bury or ignore this crisis most of the time. It's the unspoken, underlying truth of our ongoing lives; we live for a little bit, we struggle to survive and then—we die.

The other type of crisis happens to us *during* life: death in the family, loss of a job, the end of a relationship, divorce, loss of fortune, war, terrorist attacks, pandemics, hurricanes, etc.

These types of crises *cannot* be avoided, run from or denied. They smack us in the face while standing in line for coffee at Starbucks. *Nope, I can't unsee or undo that shit.* Pretty obvious. Pretty blatant.

The lesson:

Any crisis—be it existential, personal, national or world—is an opportunity to discover *that in us which is untouched by crisis*...to discover that empty, clear, internal presence which is always there, always free and always okay.

There is, indeed, something going on behind the scenes of life that most are not privy to. It is this: The universe is calling for us human beings to wake-the-fuck-up. And the best way for the universe to achieve this end..? Crisis.

Enjoy the ride.

CHAPTER 20
MINI GOLF ANYONE ?

*How to Handle earthquakes
in your brain*

I understand the need for—or I should say the human propensity for entertainment distraction. I mean, who doesn't want a break from all this shit now and again, right?

But, what I find puzzling is the need for distraction *while* you are being distracted. And of course, there can even be a third layer to this insanity if you involve your phone.

Take for instance *The Outer Banks National Seashore*. It's littered with half a dozen or so tacky, wildly-themed mini golf courses. I'm talking life-size volcanoes and pirate ships and some of the butt-fucking ugliest Tyrannosaurus Rexes you'll ever lay eyes upon.

We need all this stuff because, well, going to the beach and enjoying the surf and sunset just isn't good enough, is it? Nope— we gotta add popping small white balls with long metal sticks into the mouths (or anuses) of fake dinosaurs to the list. And of course while we're doing this, we can use our phones to order pizza and ice-cream for delivery—I shit you not—*to the fucking mini golf course!*

Is it any wonder human beings are so spiritually bereft and unaware? With distraction friends like these, who in the fuck needs enemies?

Of course, there is also the indisputable, undeniable and somewhat uncomfortable truth that the darkly humorous entertaining content of this very paragraph *is also* a distraction.

But I digress.

Your guide is driving.

After all that torture, he'd better be driving, you think.

It's an odd sight, actually...seeing him at the wheel. He's relaxed, at ease and focused. You turn around and there in the backseat is Lenny, apparently freed from the prison confines of his cat carrier. He, too, looks carefree stretched out on his favorite branch, like nothing ever happened or will happen...*ever again.*

You remember the bar fight and the prison and the hospital. *Thoughts, thoughts, thoughts*, you think.

"Penny for your thoughts?" your guide asks.

"Ha!" You burst out laughing.

"There's no way to stop them, is there?"

"Stop what?"

"Thoughts."

"Oh, those. No, there isn't. No way to stop breathing either. Once you see that thoughts and breathing are pretty much exactly alike, the thoughts stop bothering you."

"I don't know if that's comforting or disconcerting," you reply.

"Immensely *freeing* if you ask me."

"I guess so."

Your guide slows the car. You recognize the campground turn off. Within minutes you arrive at your campsite.

Shit, we were gone all night. Everything looks intact.

"Okay, so here's the agenda for the day. Beach and rest and maybe later today or tonight, if you're up for it we'll go play some mini golf."

"Mini golf? Really?"

"I know, I know it sounds silly, but trust me—it'll be fun. Get your mind off everything."

"Okay. Whatever," you grumble.

"You get some sleep. Lenny hasn't seen the ocean this trip yet. I'm going to take him to the beach and let him swim."

"Swim!?"

"Yeah, loves it, if the surf's not too rough. Back in an hour or so…"

"Have fun."

You watch as your guide wraps Lenny around his neck and saunters off toward the boardwalk leading to the beach. You sigh, then crawl into the tent and lie down. Exhausted, you're out cold in a manner of minutes.

In your dream, you're riding a horse through the jungle. All around you the verdant green, lime and chartreuse foliage dances joyfully as you ride past. You are surrounded by both cacophony and serenity. Birds, bugs, frogs and other croaking, squeaking and squawking things make their presence known... loudly. Behind it all, however—oddly enough—resides a tranquil, calm and quiet presence.

Suddenly you realize you are no longer riding a horse. It's something else! You can't tell exactly, but it's...green. You lean forward and down, trying not to fall off, to catch a glimpse of the thing you are on. It's Lenny!!

You laugh and shrug it off as normal. Your trek continues. The jungle keeps humming and buzzing. You continue to be lulled by the sounds. But soon, all you can hear is the deafening beautiful *silence* behind everything.

Oh, so inviting! It calls...beckoning you to come along. A deep pool of tranquility luring you in. Deeper and deeper, you long to dive into its warm embrace. Falling. Falling. Into the silence. The stillness. The heart of all things forever pulling you in and suddenly...

Boom! A horrible gut-wrenching rumble emanating from nowhere and everywhere simultaneously...and the earth starts shaking.

You can barely hold onto Lenny. You fall off. Lenny leaps away. Trees begin falling all around you. Dirt and rock and root and plant and grass fly everywhere. A split in the ground opens, its maw threatening to swallow you whole.

You stumble, fall and slip. It has you! It has you! It has you!

You wake up, sweat dripping off your back and shoulders. You hear a singsong whistling a few feet away. Your guide is just outside the tent and doing something. You sit up.

Fuck, you think. *What a dream...*

"You awake in there, sunshine?"

"Yeah, give me a minute," you call out hoarsely.

"No hurry. Water is awesome. Calm and warm today. You gotta get in."

"Oh cool. How'd Lenny do?" you ask, eyeballing through the tent the very creature that you were riding bareback moments ago—in a jungle— during an earthquake.

"He had a blast! Most people don't know that iguanas are natural swimmers. He even had a fan club. People stopped to take pictures."

Cool. You smile. *"Out in a minute."*

You decide that a swim would be a good thing and put on your bathing suit. You exit the tent and, after a few more words with your guide, head toward the beach.

"When you get back, you want to head out to Mount Vesuvius?" he asks as you're walking away.

"Mount Vesuvius?" You look at him, questioning.

"Mini-golf."

"Oh, right...sure—why not?" you answer and keep walking.

"You're gonna love it! It's volcano-earthquake themed!"

You stop, turn around again, and ask in disbelief, *"Say again!?"*

"Volcanoes and earthquakes. It's hilarious!"

No-fucking-way. You think and walk off to the beach.

You return from the beach, refreshed and relaxed. The ocean instantly washed the coincidence of the dream and mini golf thing far out to sea. You arrive at the camp, a little hungry but with some energy reserve.

"So, what say we get some lunch and then play some mini golf?"

"Sure," you respond.

Within a few minutes, you head out with your guide and Lenny. Kindly, he offers to drive again. You head north on Highway 12 and stop at the first little sandwich deli you see. After lunch you continue north again to *Mount Vesuvius.*

As you pull into the parking lot, your eyeballs are raped by the ugliest, silliest looking fake volcano you've ever seen— complete with some sort of water or lava flow and smoke billowing out the top.

You comment, *"It looks like a pile of smoking poop."*

"Yeah, it's mighty cheesy, but loads of fun."

You chuckle. Your guide parks, grabs Lenny and hops out.

"Okay look, the trick to this is to just turn off your critical brain and have fun."

You understand and smile in acknowledgement.

Brain off.

Oh, and right… just awareness…is left.

188

Okay—cool.

You go to the counter, pay for tickets and gather the accoutrements needed for the game...a bag of balls and two golf clubs for putting, apparently. The young college aged clerks, overly serious about their jobs, fuss around sizing you for the right club. They eventually decide that a 36" heel-shafted mallet putter is what you need. Of course, you notice that all the putters look like 36" heel-shafted mallet putters. You laugh inside and walk off to begin the game.

Your guide and Lenny have already started attracting attention. People keep approaching to fawn, to pet and/or to take selfies with the lizard.

Lenny's a fucking rock star, you think.

A mindful rock star!

The game begins and, sooner than expected, you are lost in its trivial details, successes, misses and triumphs. It's a blast and sweet relief from all the recent bullshit you've been dragged through.

At hole 9, you come into your stride. You've been under par for the last two holes and are thinking you just might be able to ride this thing out and actually win. But then your guide turns to you and says, "It's eruption time! Be aware of—awareness!"

And just that moment, *Mount Vesuvius* erupts. A huge boom sounds through the outdoor PA system; large amounts of black smoke billow out its top; and "lava"—or whatever it is—begins streaming down its side. And then...the ground beneath you starts shaking *violently*.

Your amusement quickly transforms into something altogether different and you think, *Awareness!? What the fuck does that have to do with anything?*

And then, you remember your dream. *It's got me! It's got me! It's got me!*

And that's when it really hits.

A searing rush of dread and utter fear course through your brain. Cold chills rush up your spine; you're rendered weak and paralyzed. Your heart starts thumping at Mach-10. Your palms are instantly sweaty and you have only one thought...

I'm dying. I'm going to die! What the fuck is going on!? I'm going to die!

Confused and bewildered, you look at your guide and then collapse to the ground crossed leg.

"It's just the volcano!" your guide says.

You see him smile and point. Then you see him recognize something in you— and he stoops down. He places both of his hands on your shoulders and looks you directly in the eyes.

"Breathe. Be aware of awareness."

You breathe and breathe again.

"Notice...awareness. "

You breathe again. You notice awareness.

"Good."

I don't want to notice awareness, you think.

"You are okay. This is good."

"Breathe...all part of the process."

You continue to breathe. You are dizzy from the death-n-doom anxiety attack...or whatever the fuck it was. It slowly, slowly...begins to recede.

"Process!?" you squeak out to your guide, still sitting.

"Yes—spiritual—congrats, you're in it now."

You give him a bewildered look.

"Just stay seated. I'll get you a Coke. A little caffeine will do you some good. You gonna be okay if I leave for a minute?

"Yeah...think so," you answer shakily.

"Okay, I'll be right back."

You look around. No one has noticed your death-n-doom anxiety attack in all the chaos, fun and amusement of Mount Vesuvius blowing. You slowly stand. You see your guide headed toward you with a Coke.

"Let's go sit down over at that picnic table."

"Okay," you nod.

You sit down and take a few sips of Coke. After a few minutes, you feel your Mach-10 heartbeat returning to a normal rhythm. Slowly, you come to your senses and begin breathing easier. Then, you look your guide straight in the eyes and mumble...

"What in the name of F-U-C-K was that!?"

Good question.

Brakes on.

(I'm talking to *you* with book in hand.)

Most people think that spiritual growth is measured in the amount of "feel-good-ness" they can accumulate. You know— all the typical fare: blissful feelings, joy, peace, meditation for long-ass periods of time, compassion, helping others, thinking good thoughts, being positive all the time, living in the now with a big fat ugly douche-bag smile on your face. All that shit.

But true spiritual growth?

True spiritual growth is measured in the number of volcanic earth-shattering mind quakes that unequivocally and irrevocably change you at the core level of heart and brain.

True spiritual growth is the stuff of bravery and courage.

True spiritual growth is when you invite something much, much larger than yourself in and then allow it to deconstruct you, destroy you and rebuild you...from the ground up.

True spiritual growth is to die before you actually die.

I know this for two simple reasons: One, I experienced it myself; Two, I've read a lot of really good books about it. One of these books is called *The Ego and the Dynamic Ground*, by Michael Washburn.

Chapter seven of this book is called *Regression in the Service of Transcendence*. I've always loved this title. It's so goddamned raw, true and badass accurate. Here's the first paragraph of that chapter:

'Virtually every religious tradition acknowledges periods of severe difficulty that sometimes precede or follow spiritual awakening. These periods are variously described as

- *the dark night of the soul,*
- *the spiritual desert or wilderness,*
- *the state of self-accusing (Islam),*
- *the great doubt (Zen),*
- *the ordeal of dying to the world,*
- *encounter with temptation...,*
- *Zen sickness,*
- *the descent into the underworld or into hell,*
- *and the death of the self.'*

He then goes on to brilliantly describe many of the stages and transitions that occur during this difficult time. Below is a paraphrased easy-to-read list of these transitions (say thank you, right brain):

- Withdrawal—*No thanks, I'll pass.*
- Alienation—*I'd rather be alone than with you idiots.*
- Disillusionment—*This is it? Really?*
- Encounter with Shadow— *Fear, death, uncomfortable emotions, ugh, ouch, groan, cry*
- Despair— *Who's gonna understand this shit?*
- Nothingness— *Depression, flatness, suicidal thoughts*
- Cataclysmic end of the world thinking and dreams— *Burn the whole fucking thing to the ground.*
- Anxiety — *On pins & needles all the time*
- Dread—*Cold chills, sweat, anxiety attack, deep fear*
- Strangeness— *Floating, eerie, blissful, apart, high*

So, there you have it. Everything you can look forward to while embarking on your own super-deluxe, wacked-out spiritual adventure.

Okay, stop!!

I can hear your argumentative refutations three hundred miles away:

Well, fuck that shit.

Why bother, then?

Is there a silver lining to it?

What's the point?

That's a nihilistic bag of shit; no thanks.

Whoa, Nelly! I signed up for this?

Alright. Alright. Alright.

(You knew I'd use that quote at some point in this book.)

Politely please shut the fuck up.

Thank you.

Here's the deal:

Of course, not all these experiences happen to all of us in the exact same way, shape, form or order as listed above. Some people may only have very mild versions of these things.

Others may be plagued severely by one or more of them for months or years.

As a rule, however, I can tell you this about most spiritual growth; at some point, at some time…it is inevitable that an earthquake or two rumbles across your brain.

These earthquakes are signs that the old you, ego-personality, is being replaced by the new you, awareness. They are normal and natural. And the new you— awareness—is unaffected by them.

Awareness remains untouched. Awareness remains okay.

Awareness remains at peace.

Awareness remains unscathed, unbothered and undisturbed.

Awareness—*the real you*—remains.

And therein lies the paradox:

The more you uncover awareness, the more it dismantles the ego personality and causes emotional, psychological and psychic earthquakes.

But that's when the *badass you*…the courageous, fearless and brave *YOU* can take over:

Bring it on, you will say.

Let's get this over with. I've come this far.

Fuck it, let's keep going.

I got this.

You can't touch this.

I am a rock.

Do not fuck with me!

Having served their purpose, all these regressive shadowy nightmarish episodes eventually recede; awakened awareness assumes the pilot's seat of your human ship. Ego-personality doesn't die; it just gets demoted to the co-pilot's seat. And afterwards, you will find yourself—relatively, mostly and without hype—free, happy, sane, healthy and whole.

"And that's all I have to say about that."—Forrest Gump.

Okay. Just one more thing…

In case you hadn't noticed, I just reduced the most sacred and profound secret knowledge, held and contained within the world's cumulative spiritual and religious wisdom traditions throughout history into a single potty-mouthed one paged cliff note.

And you just read it.

Damn. I'll fist-bump ya to that shit.

Okay…back to the mini golf course.

Never in your wildest dreams would you have thought that *Mount Vesuvius* 18-hole mini golf course and the sticky, old, worn picnic table with proclamations of love (and other things) carved all over it by *Derek-n-Cindy* would be the setting for your grand entrance into authentic spiritual growth.

Alas, there's just no accounting for bad taste—even in the deepest matters of the universe, soul and spirit.

Fuuuuuck.

It took about fifteen minutes for your guide to bring you up to speed—to answer and explain your most recent and profoundly philosophical question:

"What in the name of F-U-C-K was that!?"

In short, you gather, it was your spiritual cherry being popped.

And in short, you also gathered...the real roller coaster ride just began.

You sit across from your guide, sipping on your Coke and gazing vacantly upwards at the ludicrous site of Mount Vesuvius ... still blowing its wad.

I am a badass, you think to yourself.

I can handle this.

I am a badass.

Spiritual Badass Lesson:

What's odd about earthquakes is that you can't just demand their presence. They show up when they wanna show up, with no consideration for whatever trivial or heroic thing you may or may not be up to at that moment. They don't fucking care.

Earthquakes are tools of evolution and sometimes evolution can be a heartless bitch. Heartless, that is, as experienced by the ego which is suffering the earthquake. Ultimately, evolution knows exactly what it's doing.

It's been my experience that earthquakes don't show up until you are good and ready and have the awareness capacity to *handle* earthquakes.

So, when the time arrives for you to experience one, just remember this profound, auspicious, super spiritual mantra: "Good shot Tiger—hole in one!"

END PART 3

Continue your adventure with J. & Lenny:
Connect, share, laugh, grow & learn
with other books, articles,
videos, courses & more...

Go here:
www.spiritualityforbadasses.com

PART 4

Ego's Your Bitch

CHAPTER 21
KNOW THYSELF

*How to know yourself, influence
people, make friends and get rich*

About 2,400 years ago someone inscribed "Know Thyself" on the forecourt entrance wall of the Temple of Apollo in Delphi, Greece. I suppose this kind of display was the ancient Greek version of a Facebook meme. No one knows for sure *exactly* who came up with this gem, but Socrates, Plato, Pythagoras and Heraclitus are just a few of the contenders. (Yeah, um, *those* guys—the founding philosophers of civilization.)

Of all the phrases you could choose to sort of, you know—kick off civilization, "Know Thyself" is not a bad one. It implies quite a bit.

Like—hey man, before we go all crazy here and populate the whole planet with millions and millions of people, let's figure out who we are first.

Or like—hey, how 'bout before we create lots of big cities and cultures and societies and religions and stuff, we...eh, I dunno... figure out who we are, exactly?

Or, um—hey, like Whoa, Nelly! Before we go and create science and medicine and industrial revolutions and nuclear bombs and stuff, maybe we...eh, should really get to know ourselves first?

So here we are 2,400 years later and we're still chewing on the "Know Thyself" bone. Yep. "Know Thyself"—Good in theory. Horrible in execution.

You may have noticed something about *Spirituality for Badasses*: It isn't a book filled with meditation techniques. It's not a book about philosophy or religion or metaphysical theory. It's not a book about praying to God or Buddha or Jesus or Mohammed. It's not even a book about enlightenment or awakening or self-realization (...bone to all you New-Agers out there).

This is a book about *knowing thyself*, in the fullest possible sense of those two words. For instance, as a matter of mere coincidence, my twelve-year-old son just popped into my office as I was writing these words and hijacked my keyboard. I'm not making this up. Here's what he wrote:

"My name is Jeremy I am the almiteE great nugget

J)))))))))))))))))))))))))))))))))"

I have no idea what an *almighty great nugget* is, but it doesn't matter...because my son *does*. He *knows*—in his own 12-year-old way—exactly *who he is*: He knows himself! He's happy, at peace, content, filled with spontaneous humor and joy and more. (I know, I know, I'm being a biased Dad here.)

...Point is: to *know thyself* is to discover that part of you which is real, authentic and true. To *know thyself* is to identify that part of you which is eternal, empty and free. To *know thyself* is to feel in your heart, blood and bones *who* you truly are, *what* you truly are, *when* you truly are and *where* you truly are. To *know thyself* is utterly, mysteriously humbling and awesome.

One of the great and paradoxical gifts gained from knowing thyself is, of course, knowing others—often better than *they* know themselves. It's both a curse and a blessing.

For the most part, when you know yourself, you've got a pretty good head on your shoulders; your life outlook is balanced and generally positive; but, then to your horror, you look around and see all the nonsensical suffering, unhappiness and drama people go through because they *don't* know themselves. It's a complete mess.

I suppose some people who know themselves can ignore this mess and I can too, to a certain extent. But eventually, it drives you a bit crazy and sooner than later, you find yourself with a mop, broom and dustpan in your hands—doing all you can to clean it up.

There are two reasons I'm prattling on about all this: One—If I haven't already killed your false notions of what this book is about, I want to make sure I do so now. This book is about "Knowing Thyself"...*knowing yourself*, pure and simple. Two—As you're about to find out in our next set of adventures, "Knowing Thyself" is an upside down backwards 105 mph roller coaster ride—with no handlebars.

It feels good to be behind the wheel, you think to yourself. Your guide is asleep next to you; Lenny is perched in his happy spot in the back seat. The remaining stretch of Interstate 40 is before you—your route to Asheville, North Carolina; this is the next pit stop on your adventure as planned by your guide.

As you drive, you observe the constant stream of thoughts being churned out by your brain. *The beach...biker bar...Lenny... crazy Aunt Betsy...what's in Asheville?...what was that anxiety attack?...Mt. Vesuvius...Yes, we should stop at Cracker Barrel...Katy Perry has a new boyfriend... okay—now, aware of awareness.* This observer role is new to you *and* unsettling. It seems to come and go in its intensity and focus.

But it's not a role. You think, observing that thought as well.

It's more like...the factory default setting. And it was there the whole time; I just failed to see it or recognize its importance.

The miles roll by. Eventually your thinking lulls into a few wispy repetitive thoughts that, like smoke in the wind, swirl for a bit and then disappear. The GPS on your guide's phone instructs you to exit the interstate. Within a few minutes you find yourself climbing a steep, winding back road up the side of a mountain. It's late afternoon and the sun's warm embrace has reached its zenith. It's slightly hot out.

"Oh, cool. We're here."

Your guide wakes up and grabs his phone. He taps it a few times and you can hear the barely audible sound of it ringing as he puts it to his ear. Someone picks up.

"Hey, we're almost at the gate..."

"...Okay, great. We'll wait for you."

He hangs up.

"Tenzin is going to meet us at the gate. Slow down, it's coming up."

You apply the brakes and round a slight curve. As you do so, the gate comes into view.

"Whoa, Nelly!" You mumble just loud enough for your guide to hear.

"Yeah, impressive...right?"

The gate is massive and ornate. *Is that Buddhist? Definitely Asian.* You pull the Jeep up and park directly in front of it. You crane your neck to get a better view.

Two pillars of raw rock granite in shades of grey-blue, burnt umber and beige stand between a two-pieced black iron gate. But what is utterly mesmerizing is the ornate metal dragon...*no, dragons*...that have been sculpted into the gate, and painted in shades of gold, emerald green, silver, red, blue and yellow. The dragons intertwine and twist in a magnificent jumble of order and chaos. Arched above the gate between the two pillars, you read the inscription: *Seven Dragons Sanctuary.*

"Is this a monastery?" you ask your guide.

"Well, yes and no," he answers. "I guess I'd call it more of a retreat or vacation spot. It's Nepalese with a modern twist." Just then, someone zips up to the other side of the gate on a small all-terrain vehicle.

"Tenzin!" Your guide shouts with a big smile on his face.

Tenzin, who looks like he's maybe in his late 30s, dismounts from the ATV...also with a big smile. You see that he's wearing a traditional maroon and gold robe. Underneath his loosely fitting robe, you can clearly make out his t-shirt.

Yep, that's definitely a Metallica logo, you think to yourself. You also notice he's wearing Keens sandals.

"Sorry about the wait," he says.

"No worries!" your guide replies.

Tenzin unlocks a padlock and then swings the massive gate open.

He waves at you and gestures, "Come on in."

You start the engine and then pull forward beyond the gate.

"I've known Tenzin for over a decade," your guide says.

You pull forward, stop and watch as your guide jumps out. He walks up to Tenzin and bows politely with hands at his heart; then both burst out laughing, and embrace in a big bear hug.

"This is Tenzin," your guide says to you.

Tenzin walks over to the Jeep and offers his hand through the window. You take it, noticing his strong muscled arm. *Is that a tattoo?*

Tenzin, in perfect English, greets you with "Welcome, friend. Any friend of J's is a friend of mine."

"Likewise. Thanks for having us."

"Lenny!!" Tenzin exclaims. He reaches into the back seat and gives Lenny a little rub on his head.

"You guys are just in time. Dinner is in about two hours. Let's get you settled and then you can join us at the drop."

"The drop?" you question.

"The drop!" exclaims J. "It's a meditation spot. Just fantastic!"

"Weather's perfect." shouts Tenzin as he mounts and starts up his ATV. "Follow me!"

J. looks at you and says, "You're going to love this place. It's magical. Oh, and now that we're certified road warrior adventure traveler friends, you can call me J."

Really?! Okay, that's different, you think.

"And you are going to shit your pants when you see the drop!"

"Cool," you reply. But inside, for whatever reason, your stomach muscles contract in slight apprehension.

The narrow gravel road meanders for another good mile, then delivers you into a large open area with numerous buildings, paths and beautifully sculpted landscaping. In the distance, you can see the bluish mountain range of the Pisgah National Forest.

Seven Dragons Sanctuary is drop dead gorgeous, you silently surmise.

About half a dozen other cars are situated in the parking lot. You see numerous individuals, some dressed in robes and some in normal western garb meandering around.

J. hops out of the Jeep and speaks with Tenzin for a moment. Eventually, the two of you and Lenny are guided by another monk to your quarters. You and J. have separate rooms in a small dorm-like building. It's cozy, comfy and perfect for a few nights stay. At least that's how long J. said you'd be here.

You lie down for a moment, but soon you hear a knock at the door.

"You ready?" It's J.

"Bring a towel and your bathing suit...and a water bottle."

"I thought we were going to meditate," you counter.

"We are. Get dressed. It's a fifteen-minute hike."

You pack your things in a small backpack, and then put on some hiking shoes. Within a few minutes you find yourself with J., Tenzin, two other monks and a couple (you presume) who also look like visitors.

"We'll walk there in silence," J. says.

"Eh, okay," you respond.

The knot in your stomach, had relaxed slightly in the dorm but now returns.

He's not telling me something, you think.

The walk through the woods on the narrow, intricate, well-worn dirt path is charming and easy to follow. The forest softly hums with the sounds of birds and insects. The trees sway in the light breeze wafting through the woods. You walk in silence, single file, until you reach the destination.

"Okay." Tenzin announces, before you can see where you've arrived. "Who wants to go first!?"

Tenzin is excited and giddy with joy.

And then you see it.

"Right, this is your first time here…" Tenzin says to you.

"Welcome to the drop!"

You've arrived at a cliff edge, a small rock bluff with several huge conifers standing guard. Below the bluff and at the bottom of the cliff about forty feet down is a strangely aquamarine blue...*is that a lake? pond? No...it's a quarry!* The quarry is massive and looks super deep. It's a stunning hidden jewel. But the thing that has you most worried isn't the quarry. It's the zipline...*oh, fuck doodle!* It's attached to one of the massive pine trees. The line extends down and across the full width of the quarry. You notice that everyone is stripping down to their bathing suits.

Oh shit! I knew it! I knew it! You look at J. He's got a cat just-ate-the-bird guilty grin on his face.

"This is the drop!?" you ask J.

"Oh, yeah! Best zipline in North Carolina!"

You watch as one of the two monks grabs the handlebar attached to a foot-long steel cable and rolling trolley mechanism. He walks it over to the cliff edge and leaps. He zips down the line holding onto the handlebars for about five seconds and then, as advertised ... drops. You watch and listen as he yelps with glee during the twenty-foot mid-air fall into the water. He splashes into the quarry and quickly resurfaces. You see him swim to a nearby sandy beach.

Tenzin, using a small, but apparently very strong fishing line, draws the handlebar trolley back up to the cliff edge. You watch with a mixture of glee and horror. The operation repeats until it's just you, Tenzin and J. left.

"Okay, which one of you wants to go next!?"

Before you can say anything, J. grabs the handlebar and says "Me!" He leaps and is off...

"But—who's gonna..?" you yell out.

"You'll figure it out!" J. calls back. Then he shouts a big "Wa-hooo!" and, half a second later, releases the handlebar, and drops into the water.

The knot in your stomach is now tighter than a bowling ball in a bank vault as Tenzin draws the handlebar back. You slowly strip down to your bathing suit.

Oh, crap. Oh, crap. Oh, crap!

Tenzin looks at you with a gentle smile and calmly says, "Take a deep breath. Just be aware. That's all you have to do."

His reassuring words trigger something. You take a deep breath and remember the body scan exercises of the past few days.

You quickly scan your whole body from head to toe—feeling and allowing everything to be just as it is.

"That's it." Tenzin speaks again. "Relax. Don't fight it. Feel your whole body. Notice your surroundings. Allow the nervousness and notice awareness. You got this."

Still scared to death, you grab the handlebars and slowly walk up to the edge.

"On the count of three. One, two, three…"

Fuuuuuuuuuuuuuuuuuuuuuuck!

You leap and it's over in a microsecond. You drop, falling, sliding and dangling in midair, with the full weight of your body held by the grip of your hands on the handlebar. You last only momentarily before your grip gives out and you release. You freefall for what seems like an eternity, straight down into the water. The water is crisp and cool. You plunge deep beneath its surface. You quickly swim to the top and, as you break the surface, you shout with an exhilaration that you can hardly hold back.

"Whoooooooohooo! Oh, my God. That was awesome!"

Everyone on shore claps—laughing, whooping and hollering with you. You swim toward the shoreline and drag yourself onto the beach. As your feet hit the sand, you notice that your legs, knees and feet are complete jelly. The adrenaline, still coursing through your body, has you in its grip. You collapse, sitting on the beach. You watch as Tenzin hurls a large wet-dry bag with everyone's clothing in it over the cliff edge. One of the other monks swims out and retrieves it.

Tenzin is the last to go and shouts euphorically as he drops into the water and swims ashore.

As he arrives, he announces with complete seriousness and with a calm tone you can hardly believe. "Okay...let's meditate."

You look at J. and say to him with meek trepidation, *"But, I've never meditated..."*

J. looks at you and responds, "Of course you have."

I'll be the first to tell you...

I don't care much for meditation. I'm also not a big fan of prayer, chanting or devotional sing-songy "Get-yer-'rah-rah'-on" stuff either. Most of it is fluff, even though on the surface many of these things may seem practical or beneficial.

Meditation often falls into this gotta-do-it-practical-beneficial category. You probably know the drill: Sit crossed leg on a pillow for half an hour or so, watch your breathing, slow your

213

thoughts and concentrate on something—or, even better—on nothing at all. Try it. Fail. Try it again. Fail again.

Most people who become any good at this type of meditation do so by sheer force of will, usually impelled by some grandiose, long-term end goal like enlightenment, mystical vision, cosmic unity or whatever. Of course most people utterly and completely fail to acquire this end goal. Oh well, next lifetime...

The modern mindfulness movement sells and prescribes meditation in a slightly more practical way—reduce stress, quit smoking, overcome anxiety, whatever. This is better, but still requires self-discipline, daily practice and ongoing maintenance. There's absolutely nothing wrong with this approach, but it's very easy to derail and return to crappy old habits.

There is, however, a meditation middle ground. You've already been exposed to it during our badass journey. If you've been paying attention at all, you are practicing it right now.

There's no supreme end goal. There's no extreme self-discipline or concentration. You can keep your eyes open. You can do it any time or place, day or night and under any circumstance. From fly-fishing to driving, to hiking, to reading, to talking, to eating, to getting drunk in a bar, to zip lining...the only meditation you ever really need is *awareness*. Once you see it, you can't unsee it. Once you recognize it, you don't unrecognize it. Once it comes into focus...it stays in focus.

The only thing preventing you from accessing this type of meditation—the meditation of simple awareness—is *you*. Demote the *ego-you* from the pilot's seat to the co-pilot's seat; allow awareness into the pilot's seat and you're done. I did this exact thing about a decade ago. I haven't really sat down to "meditate" since then. Why? Because I'm *always* "meditating." Sounds grandiose, but it ain't.

Allow me to put all this in much simpler terms: When ego becomes your bitch, game over. Congratulations! You're now a genuine Spiritual Badass Meditation Master.

Okay. Okay, I can hear you loud and clear. *But. but, but—how do I do that? What's the process or technique?*

Got ya covered:

You don't *do* anything. You *undo.* You don't *add.* You *subtract.* You don't improve or self-help or empower or get shinier or happier or bigger or better. Nope...none of that.

You dismantle.

You disintegrate.

You dissolve.

You melt.

All of this happens to the *ego-you* until there's nothing left but awareness.

And yes, *ouch*, this process stings a little. But you're used to a little stinging, right?

Tenzin opens the wet-dry bag and then hands everyone their perspective towels, clothes and personal things. Everyone except you seems to know the routine here. After getting dressed, everyone circles up around an old fire pit, sitting in no particular way.

You do the same and sit fidgeting, trying to get comfortable.

Freefall Exercise

Tenzin speaks softly.

"Okay, guys—take a few deep breaths and get settled. Nothing to do here, right? All is welcome. All is good. Nothing to avoid or run from. Let it all show up."

"You can close your eyes or maintain eye contact with me, whichever makes you most comfortable. Take a moment to feel your body. Breathe. Be aware. Simply notice everything that's going on in the body."

You decide to close your eyes, to hide your own internal awkwardness.

Yeah, this is awkward and, oh, right...I'll just allow it. Aware of feeling awkward. Okay, cool.

"Place your attention on your toes, feet and ankles. Breathe.

"Place your attention on your shins, calves and knees. Breathe.

"Place your attention on your thighs, where they connect to your knee, the middle and where they connect to your hip. Breathe."

Oh, it's the same thing as before. I can do this.

"Place your attention on your pelvis, genitals and bottom. Breathe.

"Place your attention on your abdomen, belly, belly button, lower back and lower spinal cord. Breathe.

"Place your attention on your chest, your heart, your upper back. Breathe."

Not much to this. Feel better now...more relaxed.

"Place your attention on your shoulders, arms, elbows, hands and fingers.

"Breathe.

"Place your attention on your neck, face, forehead, scalp and top of the head.

"Breathe.

"Lastly, place your attention on your entire body. Breathe."

Got it.

"Okay gang, probably best to close your eyes for the visualization part."

Tenzin chuckles.

"Should be easy, given what we all just did.

"In this visualization, we begin by holding hands. I'll hold your hand for a little while and then, as you get comfortable, I'll let go and you'll be on your own."

Uh, hold hands? Oh...I get it. It's just pretend.

"Together, hand in hand, we walk through a rough, boulder-strewn desert environment. Permutations of natural brown, orange, red and green colors splash over the landscape. We follow a single-track light brown dirt path through some scrub, rocks and dry vegetation. The path winds around and down for a little while. Eventually, we arrive at a vast overlook and cliff edge.

"Together we stand hand in hand at the edge of a tremendously deep ravine. The ravine is so deep it's impossible to see bottom. As we peer over the edge, we see the light diminish into pure blackness. We are at the edge of the unknown itself. We are at the edge of complete mystery. We are at the edge of one way of life and the beginning of another.

"Together we are going to jump off this cliff edge. We shuffle our feet closer and closer to the rim. Small pebbles crunch, give way, and spill over and down. Close your eyes. Take a deep breath. On the count of three—we are going to jump.

"One.....Two....Three...

"Together we jump. Our stomachs flutter deeply and hearts jump to our throats as a sensation of complete freefall overtakes us.

Oh shit, we just did this. I actually kinda feel it! This is bizarre! Oh, man..!

"The air rushes by. We can see the side of the cliff zooming past us in a great blurry whirl of form and color. The sound of the air rushing through our limbs and bodies and ears is constant. We settle into this freefalling state. We surrender all control and effort. We are helpless in this state of complete freefall.

"Slowly you relax and allow the falling to completely take you...deeper and deeper you relax... to the point where you are now enjoying the complete freedom, peace and effortlessness of the fall. There is complete acceptance of the falling. Deep acceptance, gratitude and freedom. You have absolutely no control. Just falling, falling, falling.

"I am now going to let go of your hand and let you freefall on your own. We'll meet a little later at the top of the cliff...I let go of your hand and you continue to fall on your own. The air rushes by, the cliff walls rush by."

Ohhhhhhh man. Feeling queasy. What the fuck?

"You now begin the descent into darkness. The light is now quickly coming to an end. Further and further you fall. It gets darker and darker. And now, you are falling in pitch black darkness. You see nothing. You have no control, no guide, no escape. You are completely alone in the freefall. You fully accept your condition and circumstance.

"You now fall into the absolute heart of awareness itself. You are completely aware of all experiences, bodily sensations, emotions and thoughts...high or low, good or bad. You are unconditionally and absolutely aware. Aware—without hesitation, reluctance, fear or reservation.

"Take a deep breath.

"Place your attention and awareness on your body.

"Notice all the aspects of your body that you love and like."

"Be attentive to the parts of your body that you love and like.

"You continue to fall...

"Now place your attention and awareness on all aspects of your body that you dislike, run from, hate or shun. Notice the parts of your body that you dislike, run from, hate or shun.

"You continue to fall...

"Take a deep breath.

"Place your attention and awareness on your emotions.

"Notice all the aspects of your emotions that you love and like. Be attentive to the emotions that you love and like.

"You continue to fall...

"Now place your attention and awareness on all the aspects of your emotions that you dislike, run from, hate or shun. Notice the emotions that you dislike, run from, hate or shun.

"You continue to fall.

"Take a deep breath.

"Place your attention and awareness on your thoughts.

"Notice all the aspects of your thoughts that you love and like. Be attentive to the thoughts that you love and like.

"You continue to fall...

"Now place your attention and awareness on all the aspects of your thoughts that you dislike, run from, hate or shun. Notice the thoughts that you dislike, run from, hate or shun.

"You continue to fall...

"Your falling has stopped.

"You have now reached bottom."

"There is just a pitch-black emptiness. There is nothing here but empty, open, clear and honest awareness. From here on out, you will always have the capability, strength and courage to place your attention and awareness on all experiences, bodily sensations, emotions and thoughts. Take a deep breath.

"You now begin rising up out of the deep dark ravine. Faster and faster you rise. The rushing air begins again. Sound returns.

"Feeling states return. Soon you begin to see the faint glimmer of light. Slowly, shadows form and you can make out the cliff wall as you ascend.

"Faster and faster you rise. The light becomes stronger. Rising and rising. You ascend the canyon ravine. You see the colors of the cliff wall rush by you in a blur.

"You can now see the sky. And now you can see the cliff edge far above you. Rising, rising. It is now fully light again. The cliff edge gets closer. You rise further and further until at last you reach the cliff edge.

"You land...whole, at peace, empty...and stand next to me.

"Together we walk back home on the narrow desert path...completely attentive and aware to all of life."

"That's it. Thank you," says Tenzin.

I am so heavy. Why do I feel so heavy? This is really a strange sensation.

"Okay, everyone can open their eyes."

You do so. *Damn*, you think. *What was that? What is this?*

"What came up?" Tenzin smiles as he looks around and asks everyone this simple question.

George, one of the non-monk guests, speaks.

"Same old same old...I suppose. I'm always okay, until the bottom. And there he is. Always waiting there for me, it seems."

"Me, too," Carolyn, his wife, wipes away some tears before speaking. "It's been almost ten years, but I can still see him, hear him, smell him."

Tenzin replies. "Since this is something that happened to you both, why don't you both share what this pain feels like in your bodies right now. George, you want to go first?"

George nods.

Tenzin continues, "Take a deep breath, notice awareness and describe what you feel."

George speaks. "Timothy is there, always with a big grin on his face. Always the same age. Whenever I see him my heart just feels like it was hit by a Mack truck."

"And right now, in this moment?" Tenzin asks.

"Right now, it feels constricted, tight, heavy. I want to cry, but can't...or won't. Cried so many times already. So heavy."

Tenzin speaks. "Okay, good—place your complete attention on the tightness, the Mack truck in your heart. Don't fight it. Allow the full weight of the truck to bare down on your heart. Okay?"

George nods again.

"Now notice awareness. Notice the space of awareness that's here and allow that space of awareness to hold the pain of your son's death."

George lets out a loud moan and begins weeping and convulsing.

"That's it. Allow that pain to be here, George. It is completely okay and welcome here."

George cries and you watch as his face softens, and his eyes shine and come to life. You are drawn into the depth of George's own experience. Strangely, you can feel what George is feeling and are deeply touched by his painful sharing. You notice your own bodily heaviness is exaggerated now. You feel dizzy with depth, stillness and oddly enough...peace.

"How do you feel now, George?"

George nods. "Better—somewhat."

Tenzin looks on compassionately toward George. "There is no getting rid of this pain, George. This pain is legitimate, true and real. You can only let it in...fully. Become fully aware of it.

"Love the pain. Love your son. And see that somehow—if only in some small way—for now, who you truly are is untouched by this pain. Who you are is free, empty and okay. And paradoxically, this aware, free *you* is fully capable of accepting and loving the *you* who is in pain."

George takes a big breath and heaves a sigh of relief. Carolyn leans over and gives him a hug. Tears still streak down her cheeks as well. You know for sure that Carolyn was taken to the same gentle depth.

"Carolyn, do wish to share?" asks Tenzin.

Carolyn replies "I'm good, but thank you. That was plenty for me, I think. I'm pretty raw right now. Thank you, Tenzin. That was just...so beautiful. This is why we came."

Tenzin looks around "Anyone else?" You tentatively raise your hand.

Tenzin looks your way. "Yes, friend, the stage is all yours."

You look around and slowly speak.

"Well, I guess I just wanted to report or share what I'm also feeling right now. It's very strange. I've never...I just feel so, um—heavy...and everything is clear...like my vision is better—or, um, something like that."

Tenzin smiles and softly chuckles.

"It's just the meditation. You're more grounded."

"Oh, okay. I guess. But my eyes..?"

"That's what happens when you deeply relax into awareness—your peripheral vision opens up. You're meditating! Good job, friend. You just experienced your first real glimpse of the dragon!"

"The what?"

"Oh, right—the dragon...you know...*Seven Dragons Sanctuary*. That's just the Nepalese way of saying, "Kudos man, you've made some progress on the path.""

You give a quizzical look.

J. looks at you and responds

"The path to knowing thyself ...the path to being real. Fist bump, yo!"

You fist bump J. and smile widely.

Holy shit, you think to yourself. *Meditating feels fucking awesome.*

Spiritual Badass Lesson:

Let's keep this simple: Meditating should *feel* good. It shouldn't be an exercise in self-disciplined drudgery. It shouldn't be about trying to get to some far off magical unattainable place. It shouldn't be snake oil for mental health problems, physical sickness, or addiction, either.

True meditation is about discovering *that which already is* and the gateway *into that* is always *that which already is*. Dive deep enough into this realm and you'll discover all sorts of hidden gems, dark creatures, fantastical beasts and ghostly beings. In other words...you'll discover your true self. How will you know if you're doing it right? When it feels fucking awesome.

One more thing:

Maybe...just maybe you've experienced what I'm talking about simply by reading this book: A slight subtle shift. You feel more in your body. You feel heavier. You feel relaxed and grounded. Your peripheral vision has expanded slightly.

Something is different.

If so...yep, that's your dragon. Kudos, amigo.

Chapter 22
Angels & Demons

*How to "meditate" and
see ego- Part I*

S o, this is J. here, your guide. It's been a while since I've spoken directly to you. I wanted to take a moment to take you behind the stage curtain and explain, if you haven't already figured it out, why I've been using several different perspectives to communicate with you in this book.

You may have noticed that it's evolved, yes?

Let's continue to use the stage play analogy, shall we? Very simply, what has happened during the course of our adventure is this:

One day, innocently enough, you were walking down the block in my section of the city. My block happens to be an entertainment, restaurant, theater section. You walked past my big ole' marquee out front and read what was posted: *New Play! Spirituality for Badasses, by J. Stewart Dixon.*

Liking the title, you thought...*Hmmm, sounds interesting. I've got some time. So sure, why not?*

So, you purchased a ticket, grabbed some popcorn, sauntered on into the theater and grabbed a seat. Thinking you would be mildly entertained for an hour or so, you waited in anticipation as the curtain was drawn.

As the play unfolds, to your horror and delight, you discover the following: This is not your usual sit-n-watch passive play—it's interactive! Not only do the actors break the fourth wall; they come down into the audience seating area and engage with you! Even worse...they encourage you to join them on stage!

You do so, and something magical happens. You have two major epiphanies: One—You actually *like* being in the play; Two—You didn't leave the "real world" to watch a play. You left a play and have now entered the real world.

What you ultimately realize as you partake in the play and watch as other patrons enter and sit down is this: *There is no going back to the real world, because you have now awakened.* The so-called "real world" was the play, the drama, the Leela—and what you are experiencing in this moment is the true reality, the true you.

So...that, in a nutshell, my friend, is the reason for the use of multiple voices or perspectives in this book. I know it seems like those perspectives have evolved. They have not.

You have.

Now, if the previous few paragraphs didn't just fuck with your mind, I don't know what will.

You hear a knock at your door. "Good morning, Sunshine."

It's J. It's early. You're under the covers, comfy in bed, back at the dorm. You roll, moan and scrunch under the covers trying your best to avoid his cheery a.m. revelry call.

Knock, knock...again.

"Wanna sleep in..." you moan.

"The morning symphony only lasts a little bit. Come on. I got some strong coffee. It's amazing."

You roll over again and sit up, groggy and with about two percent of the enthusiasm that J. has, you whisper, *"Be out in a min."*

"Cool."

About fifteen minutes later, you're walking next to J. across the *Seven Dragons* campus with a large thermos of strong black coffee in your hand. You're wearing a rain jacket because the weather ain't great today. A light rain is pattering down from a solid, low, joy-sucking ceiling of grey clouds.

Oddly enough, however, you slowly perk up as you meander across the campus...not from the caffeine and not from the walk. Contrary to the clouds, drizzle and low light, you hear it loudly and clearly—and it's infectious: the morning symphony.

Hundreds of birds are joining in a dawn chorus of trills, flutters, chirps, cheeps and sing-song melodies. They are oblivious to the weather.

You continue the walk and arrive at the forest edge along the southern rim of the campus. There, an entrance path and sign beckon you into the forest. The sign reads *Angel Falls* and a small red arrow points into the forest.

With J., you walk into the birds' realm. Due to the canopy of leaves far above you, the patter of the rain softens immediately.

You remove your rain jacket hood and are stunned. The power, beauty and haunting delight of the morning bird symphony is overwhelming. It's divine, sonic poetry, direct from the womb of Mother Nature herself. It is a gift given...

"Fucking and fighting."

"What!?" You can't disguise your surprise.

"Fucking and fighting."

You cast a ...*Really!?* look at J.

"Most of the birds singing right now are males. And they're interested in only two things: attracting a mate, um—fucking, or warning other males to stay away— fighting."

"Well, that's depressing," you reply.

"No, it's the truth, and that response is exactly why we're here this morning. When ego hears the truth, it gets depressed, runs away, gets angry, hides, denies, isolates, walls off...or some combination of those."

You sigh.

"So this isn't going to be a leisurely stroll, is it?"

"Nope."

"Okay..."

You breathe deeply and take in the bird sounds again, the magic now somewhat dampened by J.s' grand "fucking and fighting" insight.

"Lay it on me."

"*Angel Falls* is about fifteen more minutes. We'll keep walking. I'll be kind, however, and entertain you with a quick story as we walk."

"Okay."

Once upon a time (1927 to be exact) the Zambezi River in Southern Africa flooded—historically, epically.

It had rained hard for weeks and, that spring, the Zambezi River flooded well beyond its usual levels. The river reached into portions of the savannah never reached before—sweeping up trees, rocks, huts, houses, people and animals, without discrimination.

Everything in its path was taken...was fodder...was disposable.

Some say what they saw couldn't have been real. Others say it was very real, and simply a result of the dire flooding circumstances. I suppose we'll never know. But we can *imagine*—yes sir, we can imagine—that barge with all those animals on it: an elephant, lions, hyenas, zebra, rabbits, tortoise, gazelles, impalas and kudus...all those animals on the same boat, floating down the river. We can imagine it and we can *imagine* their story...

Somehow, and who knows exactly how, the elephant was able to climb aboard first. The barge was about twenty-five feet long, fifteen feet wide, flat and, most importantly, buoyant. The elephant didn't know it but the barge had been used to ferry cars and trucks—one at a time—about nine miles up-river. Dislodged from its moorings in the fury of the flooding, the barge had floated all the way down river to the elephant's territory.

He stood afraid and cold as the barge careened uncontrollably down the swollen river. Little by little the others joined him. It was no big deal when the zebras boarded. And it was no big deal when the impalas and kudos hopped on. No one cared about the tortoise, either; he was relatively small and stayed tucked inside his shell. But having the lion and lioness jump on—well, this was disconcerting.

231

Regardless, others still boarded even after them, the risk of close proximity to a pair of lions outweighing the certain death of the sweeping flood waters.

But this story isn't about the wild coincidence of a group of animals bucking the food chain law of the jungle during a flood. This is a story about *the barge*. Because you see, those animals, not knowing any better, stayed on that barge well after the rains had stopped and the flooding had gone down.

Every last inch of that barge now held a cowering, hungry and grumpy animal, reptile or insect. It had become a festering, stinking, walled-off and isolated death trap. They were all standing in their own shit. The barge was filled well beyond weight capacity. It was only a matter of slight chance or time before the whole thing capsized.

And then they saw it—and they all knew.

That fly was headed directly toward them. The barge could hold no more, not even the weight of a single African black fly. The buzzing got louder and louder. All the animals held their breath and prayed that the fly wouldn't land, wouldn't see them, wouldn't rock their precious barge—the barge which had saved them, the barge which was now their world, the barge which was all that stood between them and...certain death.

But it was not meant to be. That fly landed.

It landed right on the back of the elephant. And the elephant swatted. And when he did, all hell broke loose.

The barge careened in the direction of the swat and violently cantilevered at a forty-five degree angle. It righted itself, but the force of the return caused several animals to go flying overboard and the force of the animals flying overboard caused the barge to cantilever again—and finally to capsize.

All aboard went into the water and

And...and...

Most of the animals simply walked to shore. Some of them swam... easily.

Because...

For days now the water had been only three feet deep; the rain had been mostly gone; the swollen river had been shrinking and returning to normal; and the barge had been...completely useless.

And, as you may have surmised, this story isn't even really about that barge.

It's about ego—very useful at first, but useless in the end. And sooner than later...a fly is going to land on it.

You and J. arrive at *Angel Falls*. It's pretty, but nowhere close to its namesake sister in Venezuela—the world's highest.

This *Angel Falls* is a small, quaint creek trickling down a natural rock embankment for about twenty feet. There's a two-seat mostly wooden bench nearby. The birds have softened their morning chorus. You look up and through the forest canopy.

You make out a few breaks in the clouds and surmise that the sun is doing its darndest to dissipate the gloom.

As you take a seat on the bench, you remark:

"That's a nice story, but I still don't have a clue what ego is. Egotistical, I understand, I guess. Ego, id, Freud. All that...no clue.

J. replies:

"That's pretty typical...most people don't understand ego, because ego doesn't *want* to be understood. It's in its best interest *not* to be understood or discovered or seen.

"Okay, but..."

"Spiritual Badasses don't have this problem. Spiritual Badasses see ego, understand it and accept it. Specifically, they accept two things about it: One—it will never go away as long as you're alive. Two—spiritual progress inevitably demotes, dismantles and renders ego harmless."

"Okay, but I still don't know what it is. What the fuck do you mean by ego!?"

J. pauses, thinks and then responds, looking you directly in the eyes.

"Don't say I didn't warn you. Close your eyes. Let's do an exercise. But first allow me to gently explain."

J. sits down next to you on the bench. You close your eyes and listen to J. speaking. In the background, you hear the soft mesmerizing trickling of *Angel Falls.*

"Okay. I'm going to be gentle here. I have to be gentle, because what's about to take place is intricate, delicate surgery. We're going in. This may hurt a little. Contrary to my other teaching, I promise, I'll try to be as kind as possible. You ready?

"Take three deep breaths. Inhale once.

"Pause. Inhale again. Pause. Inhale again. Pause.

"Let's start with a simple definition of ego that adequately served me while on the spiritual path. Ego is my sense of identity: J. Stewart. Me. I. J.s' habits, desires, personality characteristics, limitations, weaknesses, insecurities, strengths, dreams, powers, skills, talents, the things he thinks about himself, and the things he thinks others think about him.

Ego as a whole is the J. *Identity Project.*

Like all human beings, the J. Identity Project is ultimately seeking love, security, comfort, peace or happiness. The J. Identity Project is seeking pleasure and avoiding pain. This project is not so much a thing as it is an *activity.*

Therefore…

Ego is the activity of doing, working, socializing, performing, talking, thinking, dreaming, desiring, and longing...all in the name of seeking pleasure and avoiding pain. Seeking. Searching. Desiring. This is the constant never-ending activity of ego.

You do it, consciously or unconsciously. You do it aware of or ignorant of—*all the time.* Ego is wrapped up in every single facet of your existence.

Ego is an *activity.*

Once you finally begin to understand *and see* this constant activity, one very salient thing about it becomes apparent: Ego never fulfills its promise.

No matter how plain, complex, ignorant, intelligent, fabulous, terrible, famous, unknown, stupendous, humble, weak, spiritual, creative, powerful—or badass— your grand ego-identity project grows to be, it never… truly… ultimately…

235

delivers. It only leaves you wanting more. You never arrive at the ultimate life of fulfillment; the ego is constantly promising.

Ego is an *activity.*

Ego is an always-dangling carrot held on a string three feet in front of you. Try as you might, you never reach the carrot. *And*—you can't stop reaching.

Pretty gloomy, right? Actually—No. Not gloomy.

If this absolute bare-bones realization of ego's dead-end, nihilistic, sadistic promise was all there was to realize—then yes, this would be some pretty fucking gloomy shit indeed.

But the good news is this: There's something else to realize. And that *something* is the very thing that *sees ego* to begin with:

Awareness. Awareness sees ego.

Awareness *precedes* ego.

This is the beautiful and magical part of the whole badass spiritual process: at the same time you see and dismantle ego, you see and empower awareness...until their roles are reversed.

Awareness no longer takes a back seat. Awareness takes the pilot's seat and ego takes the back...co-pilot's seat.

This reversal of roles introduces a revolution in your life and in many ways becomes the defining feature of being a spiritual badass .

A few final thoughts and then we'll move on to the exercise. In seeing ego, we are not bashing ego. There is no judgment going on here; I have no problem with ego. You need ego to function in this world. As a matter of fact, in a paradoxical way, ego needs to be your best friend—because you need its badass strength: To transcend or completely see the ego, you must have a big enough ego to think that you can actually transcend it. Go figure.

So again, ego is not the enemy. Your identity project is not bad. It is simply limited in its ability to deliver. Thus, it is of vital importance that you see ego and all its limitations.

Ego is an *activity*.

Seeing Ego Externally Exercise

An odd thing happens while J. speaks to you. You return to the heavy, open-eyed "meditating" experience you had the day before at the drop.

The sobering truth. The sobering truth..?

Then the insight hits you: The sobering truth, like George and Carolyn's sharing of their grief about their son and this sobering truth about ego, somehow causes...stillness, depth, heaviness or ...meditation. No effort. No force. No trickery. Just the sobering truth.

Weird. This depth.

J. continues:

"We'll do a very brief body-scan."

"Place awareness on your body.

"Notice your toes, your feet, your ankles, your shins, your knees, your thighs. Breathe deeply.

237

"Notice your groin, your lower back, your stomach, your mid-chest, your heart, your upper back. Breathe deeply.

"Notice your shoulders, your arms, your elbows, your hands, your fingers. Breathe deeply.

"Notice your neck, your face, your forehead, your scalp and the top of your head. Breathe deeply."

You relax...and the "meditation" goes deeper as you do the body-scan.

"Place your attention and awareness on your whole being during this exercise. As you listen to the words I'm about to communicate, let them resonate in your heart and body. Breathe deeply. If you feel resistance to these words—notice the resistance, allow it, embrace it and let it go. Resistance is completely normal, natural and okay. Simply see that you are not the resistance—you are not the fear. You are the awareness that precedes and perceives the fear and the resistance."

Seeing Ego in The Universe

"The Universe is infinite, which makes it a realm—not a place. And just like a dream, the Universe has no edges or boundaries in time or space. The primary law in the Universe is this: For every action, there is an equal and opposite reaction. This is the first law of thermodynamics and in oriental philosophy, the Tao. What this law means for you is that no matter how hard you try or how sophisticated your efforts are, ego will never attain complete fulfillment.

"The Universe is limited and conditional. There has never been a time in this Universe when complete ego fulfillment was possible. There will never *be* a time. Simply put, this entire

238

Universe is a *learning* realm. It will never be the paradise that ego promises.

"Release the fantasy that the world—the Universe—will someday in the future be a perfect paradise. Release the delusion that life in the past, either a hundred years or a thousand years ago, was somehow better. Release the delusion that life in the future will somehow be better.

"The Universe and the laws that govern it will always be the same. Release the Universe as a place to gain fulfillment. Relax and embrace the Universe as a dream realm and, paradoxically, you will awaken to the fulfillment you were seeking.

"Think of the Universe now; be aware and mindful while you are doing this. Lovingly let it go. Lovingly see and feel how this Universe fails to truly fulfill.

"Who are you before the Universe? Who are you after the Universe? Who are you now?

J. pauses, then says, "I'm going to keep going here. Okay? Just relax and go along for the ride."

Seeing Ego in The World and Society

"The world—along with the people who inhabit it, the governments which run it, and the ideologies which guide it— is an imperfect place. There is no perfect country. No perfect policy. No perfect government. No perfect political party. No perfect society. No perfect religion. No perfect philosophy. No perfect spirituality. No perfect race, skin color, tribe, ethnicity or way of life. All of it is limited. All of it is conditional. Ego demands certain conditions for fulfillment to occur. Ego demands the right country, the right political party, the right president, the right religion, the right church, town, time and place to be fulfilled.

"Let this go. There is great wisdom in allowing the world to be exactly the way it is: seemingly imperfect, flawed and broken. Paradoxically, it is when we let go of our efforts to control, manipulate, enforce, coerce, improve or change the world that it becomes a better, lighter, and freer place—that *we* become better, lighter and freer.

"Let the world go and you will awaken to the fulfillment you were seeking all along. Think of the world and society now— be aware and mindful while you are doing this. Lovingly let them go. Lovingly see and feel how the world and society have failed to truly fulfill.

"Who are you before the world? After the world? Who are you now?"

Seeing Ego in Family and Friends

"Seeing ego in family and friends means that you begin to see all of the ways in which your ego identity project is grasping, clinging, manipulating, and seeking fulfillment through those with whom you are most intimate.

"Perhaps you are seeking to have your parents understand, respect or admire you. Perhaps you are longing for your siblings to be more like you. Perhaps your cousins need to act more responsibly. Perhaps your husband does not listen or your wife does not participate. For ego—there is always something wrong with family, something that needs changing, improving or fixing. Ego never accepts them just the way they are. Ego does the same with friends.

"There is no perfect parent. There is no perfect grandparent, brother, sister, aunt, uncle or cousin. There is no perfect family. There is no perfect friend, friendship, or group of friends. Our families and friends are limited, flawed and imperfect. Seeing ego in family and friends implicates all.

"Upon seeing your ego, you begin to see the ego of others—including family and friends. You soon begin to see that all egos are simply doing the best they can. They, too, are seeking and longing for fulfillment and love. With this seeing comes great compassion and the truest understanding of human nature."

"Let your family and friends go and, paradoxically, you will awaken to the fulfillment you were seeking through them all along. Think of your family and friends now—be aware and mindful while you are doing this. Lovingly let them go. Lovingly see and feel how family and friends have failed to truly fulfill.

"Who are you before family and friends? Who are you after family and friends? Who are you now?"

Seeing Ego in Sexuality

"Seeing ego in sexuality means seeing the failure of sex to bring true lasting fulfillment. Seeing ego in sex is simply seeing the limitation of sex and accepting it. Seeing ego in sex is to let go of our neurotic, grasping and never-ending desire for fulfillment though sex.

"Let me be very clear here: There is nothing inherently wrong with sex. Sex is not bad. But it is very common for egos to rely solely on sex for fulfillment. Seeing ego in sex is to release it from the bonds of this unrealistic fulfillment expectation.

"There is no perfect sex. No perfect sexual partner. No perfect amount of sex. No perfect place for sex. No perfect kind or form of sex.

"Let sex go and, paradoxically, you will awaken to the fulfillment you were seeking through sex all along. Think of sexuality now—be aware and mindful while you are doing this. Lovingly let it go. Lovingly see and feel how sex has failed to truly fulfill.

"Who are you before sex? After sex? Who are you now?"

Seeing Ego in Work and Play

"Seeing ego in work means seeing the failure of a career, work or job to bring true lasting fulfillment. Seeing ego in work is simply seeing the limitation of work and accepting it. Seeing ego in work is to let go of seeking fulfillment through work."

"There is no perfect job, work or career. No perfect place to work. No perfect time to work. No perfect boss. No perfect employees. No perfect co-workers. No perfect salary. No perfect hourly rate. No perfect monetary compensation.

"Work does not ultimately fulfill. Work is conditional.

"Seeing ego in play means seeing the failure of a hobby, pastime or passion to bring true lasting fulfillment. Seeing ego in play is simply seeing the limitation of play and accepting it. Seeing ego in play is to let go of seeking fulfillment through play. There is no perfect hobby, pastime or passion. No perfect sport. No perfect art. No perfect project. No perfect creativity. No perfect movie, book, play, festival or party.

"Let work and play go and, paradoxically, you will awaken to the fulfillment you were seeking through work and play. Think of work and play now—be aware and mindful while you are doing this. Lovingly let it go. Lovingly see and feel how work and play have failed to truly fulfill.

"Who are you before work and play? After work and play? Who are you now?"

J. stops talking.

While he was speaking, you settled into a place of incredible stillness and sobriety. Nothing more is said as you both sit in silence, gazing upon the idyllic forest waterfall and its surroundings.

During the "meditation," the sun played hide and seek with the clouds. Now, the sun has won the game and shines down through the treetops—illuminating leaves, rocks, grass, sticks and branches. The freshly drenched environment glistens with the sun's new rays. You are amused by the irony of the light defeating shadow.

All is well. All is still.

Without warning...Snap! Bang! Horror!

Not in the forest surroundings but from somewhere deep within—*Oh fuck!* Another brain earthquake. The anxiety and fear overtake you in an instant. Chills overtake you. You tremble and look around for an escape. There is no goddamn escape!

I have to go hide in my room!

Then tears. Scared to death and near out of your mind, you shout loudly while convulsing:

"Fuck you, Dad! Fuck you for leaving! You drunk, fucking, belligerent asshole!"

The tears pour. The outburst shocks you, but you are helpless.

More crying. More convulsions. Your body contracts. You can barely breath. You sob and moan.

"Fucking son-of-a-bitch."

You look up at J. in wild teary-eyed bewilderment.

"I have no idea where this is coming from."

"It's okay. I do." says J. "Part of the game. Stuff like that can stay buried deep sometimes …and for a long time. This work tends to draw it out."

"But I thought I dealt with…"

"Yeah, a lot of us think that. You okay? Best to let it all out."

"Not now. That was plenty."

You manage a tepid smile.

"That was some crazy fucking shit. I thought I dealt with that…"

You pull yourself together somewhat—and slowly stand. Knees wobbly and body coursing with adrenaline, you walk around a bit and take a few deep breaths. It takes a few minutes for you to calm down. The tears dry. The convulsions stop.

"Have a drink." J. offers you his water bottle. You take it and down a few swigs.

"You wanna head back?"

"I think so...yeah."

"Before we do, try something. It will make you feel ten times better. Take your shoes off and stick your bare feet in the water. Your hands and face, too, if you can stand it."

With nothing to lose, you give it a whirl. Shoes off and barefoot, you walk over to the stream pool just below the falls. You stick your feet in. Immediately, your body comes to attention and returns to focused solid ground.

Oh, shit. Aaaaaaaah...

It's fucking miraculous how good it feels. You quickly bend over and brave the rest. Leaning down, you dunk your head—all of it—in the deep pool of ice-cold water. You emerge and shout.

"Whoooo-hoooo!!! Holy shit, that's better."

You turn to J. *"How'd you know!?"*

J. looks at you with a twinkle in his eye, and says with perfect timing and unapologetic charm: "Must be...all the angels."

Spiritual Badass Lesson:

To make ego your bitch, you must see it. What sees it is awareness. When awareness sees ego, it denudes it, calms it and, in general, reduces its negative impact.

Sounds simple...but for most, it's not. It gets complicated quickly because ego wants to survive at all costs. Ego is also devilishly resourceful at hiding shit and does so throughout your life. Ego hides wounds, traumas, unhappiness and all sorts of toxic experiences deep within the layers of body, mind, emotion and thought. It can be a muddy mess in there.

Go mucking around in the core parts of that ego mud and you start to disturb the muck. Even if you think you've already dealt with your muck, you probably haven't...at least on the level required to be a spiritual badass.

Ego is something all spiritual badasses have to contend with. The good news is this however: A healthy ego is usually required to *transcend* ego. Being that you already have some spiritual badass in you...you probably have a fairly healthy ego. So, your chances of success are much higher than most.

Don't get cocky, kid.

(I can't remember- Have I used this Han Solo *Star Wars* quote already?)

CHAPTER 23
SPIRITUAL BYPASSING

How to "meditate" and see ego- Part 2

Probably one of the most famously talked about, but largely unread, western psychology/eastern philosophy books ever written was published in 2000 and titled *Toward a Psychology of Awakening: Buddhism, Psychotherapy, and the Path of Personal and Spiritual Transformation,* by John Welwood.

You may not have heard of this book, but maybe you've heard its most widely recognized term, *spiritual bypassing.*

Welwood defined spiritual bypassing as using "spiritual ideas and practices to sidestep personal, emotional 'unfinished business,' to shore up a shaky sense of self, or to belittle basic needs, feelings, and developmental tasks."

I can't tell you the number of people I have met guilty of this spiritual faux pas. I would rank it as *the number one* most common trap that spiritual seekers and aspirants have fallen into throughout history.

If the devil had to come up with one sure-fire bullet to prevent believers from getting into heaven, he couldn't do much better than spiritual bypassing.

Allow me to help you understand what *spiritual bypassing* means by providing you with this handy dandy, easy-to-read, quick start guide and analogy:

Imagine a hoary old professor outside at night pointing to the stars. He waxes philosophical and poetic about nebulae, galactic equatorial lines, planetary alignments and astrometric binary star clusters.

You're impressed.

He's standing next to an $18,000 Meade 16" LX600 ACF Telescope with a Star-Lock system mounted on a Super Giant Field Tripod. (Thank you, Google.)

You're even more impressed.

He then whips out his astrophysics undergraduate degree, PhD, doctoral dissertation and finally...his Penguin Random House New York Times best seller, *"Space is Cool and Really Turns Me On."* You see Nedley Yavonovich printed below the picture on the front cover and assume you're face to face with Dr. Yavonovich himself.

You are really fucking impressed now —with everything except his name.

He opens the book, signs it, moves a few steps closer to you and hands it over, introducing himself and his book. As he does so, you notice something about Nedley that you, um, hadn't noticed before...

Nedley is wearing stained yellow and brown diapers and is standing in a pile of his own feces as he is speaking with you. With this realization your previously mute olfactory senses, suddenly kick in, and are immediately, *deeply* offended.

You are no longer impressed with Nedley. You drop the book and run away, screaming into the night.

You are now forever traumatized by diaper-wearing, book-wielding astrophysicists and will never again, for the rest of your life, get near a telescope.

Nedley Yavonovich has just provided you with an excellent example of *spiritual bypassing*: Shooting for the stars, while standing in a pile of your own shit.

You return with J. to the campus. Nothing much is planned for the day, so you spend it meandering around the grounds, peeking inside various buildings, and having the occasional polite conversation with other guests, monks and a few members of the grounds crew.

Internally you are grateful for the time and space. A lot has happened in a very short time, and it feels like parts of you are playing catch-up. Mostly, you are just relieved to be able to turn your brain off.

At one point you see J. out for a stroll with Lenny wrapped around his neck. You recall the biker bar, and the jail, and the hospital, and the beach. *Was that just last week? It's all a blur. What a ride—and we aren't even there yet, wherever there is?*

And then you catch yourself, because...how could you not at this point? Aware of those thoughts. Aware of walking. Aware of the environment. Aware of sounds... sights ... smells ... tastes ... feelings. *Aware of it all.*

And then it also hits you. *There*—is always here! There is no there. There is only *here and now*. When tethered to awareness, you are always in the present *here and now* moment!

Holy fuck!! This is like some serious Zen shit! I gotta...I gotta tell J.!

You then laugh internally at the thought of presenting your grand Zen insight to J. in a place called *Seven Dragons Sanctuary*—home to about a dozen seasoned Nepalese monks...monks who've probably had more insights collectively than Freud, Jung and Plato combined.

You smile.

You let it go. You let it *all* go and are giddy with joy at the mere fact of discovering —the fucking present moment.

Ha!

Ridiculous, you think.

Like, I'm dying of thirst. Sooooo...thirsty. Need... a ...drink.

And meanwhile, all along, right next to you is a clear mountain stream.

Oh, man. Crazy.

The day passes. You grab lunch in the dining hall. You take a nap. You meander. You think about things. You don't think about things. You smile. You get bored. It's a day. It's actually...a really *great* day.

And then evening arrives.

Oh, Fuck.

You and J. have been invited to the evening get together in the meditation hall. You don't know what is meant, exactly, by "get together," but you are worried.

Worried—because you are feeling a little vulnerable. Worried—because just this morning you experienced yet another earthquake. Worried—because this unfinished business with your father has spooked you. Worried—because you're unsure if you're *really ready* for this shit, even though you're *already*...in the shit. And anyway, just how much *more* shit can you handle?

Shit. Shit. Shit.

It's after dinner now—6:50 p.m.; J. knocks on your door. With a sense of foreboding and dread, you open the door and put on your best fake smiley face.

"You ready?"

"Yeah, one sec."

You grab your jacket and then shut the door behind you.

"This should be kind of cool, don't you think?" says J.

"Yeah, sure," you squeak out.

"Hmmm?" J. looks at you directly. "You're nervous, aren't you?"

"Yeah."

Long pause.

"A little."

You both exit the dorm and head across the worn moss-covered red brick pathway leading to the meditation hall.

"Let me give you a quick thirty-second tip about nerves, fear and dealing with your own internal stuff...okay?"

"But I…"

"Trust me. No matter the circumstance…this is worth its weight in gold. Alright?"

Another long pause.

"Okay."

"Here it is." J. takes a big breath before speaking.

"Concerning matters of spiritual growth and discovering your own badass true aware self …There is no amount of bad-scary dark-shadowy shit you can't handle. Why is this? Because all that shit comes up *as a result of and in response to* your own badass true aware *self-growth*."

"What this means is that when bad shit gets stirred up inside you and starts rising to the top, it's because you've now given birth to, created, empowered and generated…enough awareness to handle it."

"In short—yes, you will be afraid. And yes, the new aware you can handle it. *Two yeses.* Remember the two yeses—*yes* to fear and *yes* to awareness—and you're golden."

"Got it?"

Long pause. You both arrive at the sanctuary doors.

"Yep."

J. opens the door.

Fuuuuuck me, you think as you both enter.

If there was ever a magical entrance anteroom into the combined realms of Narnia, Shangri-La, Hogwarts and Middle Earth—the *Seven Dragons Sanctuary* meditation hall would totally qualify.

Architecturally, it's a fifty by fifty foot room with twelve-foot ceilings and numerous circular, fluted, white floor to ceiling columns sprinkled throughout. The room is softly lit with a mixture of modern LED light and flickering candlelight.

The avalanche of deliberately and delicately arranged modern art pieces, paintings, statues, wall hangings, mandalas, thangkas, candles, incense burners, prayer flags and small bells is immense. But what really knocks you to your knees and melts your heart is the ambient sound and feel of the place...

Walking into the *Seven Dragons Sanctuary* is like returning to the womb. The wall to wall maroon carpet dampens all sound and foot travel. The incense wafting through the air grabs you in its smoky embrace and doesn't let go...melting you and uniting you with the room.

And then, the pièce de résistance: Music, unlike anything you've ever heard, emanates from hidden speakers and washes over the whole place. It isn't cheesy, religious, Hindu, Buddhist chanting crap either. It's modern, elegant, tasteful...ambient electronica. Something you'd more likely encounter at a *Burning Man* festival than in a traditional Nepalese Buddhist temple.

This place rocks, you think.

Tenzin is here. You see him walk over from one corner of the room. He approaches and, with hands at his chest, bows slightly to both you and J.

He smiles and greets you: "Take off your shoes and come on over."

You and J. remove your shoes and then follow Tenzin over to the corner.

Damn! you think as you arrive at a funny little circle of about a dozen or so cheap plastic bucket seats—oddly out of place in the hall. But your internal exclamation isn't about the cheap chairs; it's about the seven statues, previously hidden by several columns, now in full view.

Standing before you, in magnificent three-dimensional relief, are the seven dragons…each about ten feet high: Three solid white marble dragons on the left, three solid white marble dragons on the right, and a single solid black onyx dragon in the center. Each completely different. Each intricate, fierce, dreamy, swirling, agile, beautiful, languid and serene. The whole thing is just breathtaking.

"Pretty damn amazing, huh?' Tenzin speaks, knocking you out of your revelry.

"Yeah, it is," you muse.

Did he just curse? you think to yourself, smiling.

"Take a seat. The others will be here soon." Tenzin says.

You and J. choose seats and settle in. J. closes his eyes. You do the same.

Within a few minutes a handful of guests and two other monks arrive. Soon, ten people are seated in the small circle of cheap plastic chairs. George and Carolyn are among them. Your nervousness, previously subdued by the beauty of the room, has returned. A few people are whispering. Some are chatting openly.

Tenzin rings a small hand chime; everyone responds with silence.

"So, tonight we have a guest speaker. This is J. and his guest." Everyone looks your way and says hi. You smile nervously.

"J. is going to lead us in a meditation and then we'll talk. J., what do you have for us?"

J. takes a big breath.

"Thanks, Tenzin. Thanks for having us on such short notice. Always a pleasure to be in this magical place."

Long pause.

J. continues.

"So let's begin by making sure our legs are uncrossed and feet are flat on the floor. Take a few deep breaths. You can close your eyes or have them open...whatever you're comfortable with."

"Briefly, let's notice our entire bodies: Feet. Bees. Eggs. Groin. Backwards, Crest. Arms. *dealer*. Necklaces. Face *and dead.*"

I'm not interested.

I can't do this.

So tire...

"Welcome it all here. Be aware of it."

"Take another big breath. Inhale and exhale."

I'm trying. Deep breath. But...

"This morning we were visiting *Angel Falls* and the subject of ego came up. I'd like to continue that theme here with *eggs on the side with waffles* about ego...and seeing it internally."

I really don't wanna...

I just...sleep. Long day. Want some waffles...Damn those are big dragons...

Fuck me if those waffles came to life...

J. looks directly at you and says loudly:

"Wake up, friend; you're bypassing." You snap immediately out of it.

Holy shit. He's right. I was falling asleep. Bypass? What was that?

You look around, slightly embarrassed. No one has noticed.

Allow the embarrassment. Oh right...Yes to fear. Yes to awareness.

"Eating, talking, thinking and emoting are cool when you are hungry, need to speak to someone, need to figure something out, feel scared about a car that just nearly hit you, excited about the game you just won, or sad about the relative who passed away."

J. takes another long pause.

"But when eating, talking, thinking and emoting become the sole cure for our existential spiritual lives, we get in trouble. When we eat, talk, think and worry as a reaction to a deep hole inside of us...that's a problem. Doing so just adds unhappiness and suffering to unhappiness and suffering."

Deep hole? Do I have a deep hole? Why was I tuning this out?

Oddly, your nervousness and sleepiness have subsided.

Strange, you think...*thought for sure I'd be in full on panic attack mode by now.*

Bypassing?

J. continues.

Hey there.

Interruption time.

Me author.

You reader.

Make fire.

Eat meat.

Snap out of it!!

Hand reaching out of the book. Slapping you in the face.

Glass of cold water. Dump.

Okay. I think I have your attention.

Yes?

You awake, Sunshine?

Cool.

Here's the reason for the interruption:

Sooner or later while on the spiritual path, you are going to bypass. There's going to be a part of the teaching that will make your eyes glaze over and your head tilt back. There's going to be some part of the teaching that you just don't have enough awareness to understand or cope with. You'll find it boring, meaningless, dry or uninteresting. You'll get stuck.

It happens. Bypassing is perfectly normal and natural. I did it. I've seen many other people do it. I've seen lots of people do it live in workshops with teachers. I've seen people do it while I was teaching. Fuck...I've seen *bad teachers* do it.

But I don't want you to do it *right now*. And I want to put the kibosh on you doing it bunches while we're on this Spiritual Badass Adventure together and while you're on your *own* Spiritual Badass Adventure. Okay?

Why is this? Because spiritual bypassing has a way of turning what should take mere months into years...decades...whole lifetimes even. When you bypass, months and years can go by with zero change.

Stuck. Stuck. Stuck. Argh!

Well fuck that shit. Spiritual Badasses get it done quickly, efficiently and with as little hassle and drama as possible. I'm creating all this hoopla about "bypassing" right now in hopes that when it hits you, you'll recognize it:

You will be bored. The teaching will seem dry, heady and not pertinent. You won't get it. You won't see the point. It has no effect on you. It's empty of juice and pizazz.

This is bypassing.

Here's how you get out of it:

Most bypassing is a result of avoiding basic internal issues and repeating the same set of outer activities (like reading, meditating, praying, positive thinking, etc.) over and over again with little to no effect.

You need to shake things up. I don't care *what you do* to shake things up, but anything is better than nothing and definitely better than the same old shit you've *been doing*. I mean, look at all the ridiculous badass crap I've dragged you through in this book! Pick one.

Go for it:

- Take a yoga class.
- Attend an online spiritual workshop or class.
- See a therapist.
- Get a deep tissue massage.
- See a shaman and micro-dose psilocybin.
- Visit a shrine, temple or church five hundred miles away.
- Visit an amusement park and get on the biggest, scariest ride.
- Go white water kayaking.
- Smoke some weed.
- Do a silent retreat for five days.
- Juice fast for a few days.
- Cry your heart out alone.
- Cry your heart out in a group.
- Start a journal.
- Get a gym membership and work out.

The point here is to *move*...in any direction except the one you're currently headed in. *Move* and you will have far fewer episodes of spiritual bypassing, boredom and stuck-ness.

Seeing Ego Internally Exercise

J. continues.

"The point here, once again, (he looks at you directly) is to understand and see that ego is an *activity*. It's always on the hunt. Always scanning and moving forward. Always seeking. Always moving. Always promising.

"Often, all this ego commotion prevents us from seeing *that* which is already present, fulfilled and okay: awareness. Here we go. Eight rounds. I'll try to be efficient."

Round one: Let em' eat cake! Rich foods:

"Cake, pies, muffins, cookies, ice cream, candy, sugared cereals, Coke, fruit drinks and more. See the element of ego which seeks fulfillment through rich foods. ...nothing evil or bad about rich foods, but when chocolate cake is covering up or numbing the hole in your heart or spirit, it must be seen. Lovingly be aware of the ego activity of rich foods. Who are you before eating rich foods? After rich foods? Who are you now? Allow awareness to see the ego activity of rich foods."

Round two: What's for dinner? Normal foods:

"Oatmeal, orange juice, cereal, eggs, ham, toast, salad, turkey, fish, broccoli, rice, pasta, tomatoes, peppers, eggplant, chicken, bananas, apples, an occasional frozen meal or fast-food meal and more. See the element of ego which seeks fulfillment through normal foods. You obviously have to eat. But when eating even normal foods is covering up or numbing the hole in your heart or spirit, it must be seen. Lovingly be aware of the ego activity of normal foods. Who are you before eating? After eating? Who are you now? Allow awareness to see the ego activity of normal foods."

Round three: Smoke break, anyone? Toxic stuff:

"Alcohol, beer, wine, cigarettes, cigars, marijuana, vapes, tobacco dip, numbing pharmaceuticals, hard drugs like crystal meth and more. See the element of ego which seeks fulfillment through toxic stuff. Certain toxic stuff is fine—in moderation. Other toxic stuff is not fine under any circumstance. Your job is to see that toxic stuff is usually covering up or numbing a hole in your heart or spirit. Lovingly be aware of the ego activity of toxic stuff. Who are you before toxic stuff? After toxic stuff? Who are you now? Allow awareness to see the ego activity of toxic stuff."

Round four: I love you all, man! Positive Emotions:

"Love, happiness, joy, laughter, serenity, peace, confidence, admiration, trust, acceptance, anticipation, interest, passion and more. See the element of ego which seeks fulfillment through positive emotions. Obviously, nothing wrong with positive emotions, but, oddly enough, positive emotions can also be used to mask, hide or numb deeper internal issues. Lovingly be aware of the ego activity of positive emotions. Who are you before positive emotions? After positive emotions? Who are you now? Allow awareness to see the ego activity of positive emotions."

Round five: Don't hate on me! Negative Emotions:

"Anger, rage, loathing, grief, terror, disgust, sadness, fear, annoyance, boredom, distraction, denial, remorse and more. See the element of ego which seeks fulfillment through negative emotions. Negative emotions serve a valid purpose. Often, however, we slip into overindulging in negative emotions. Negative emotions very often hide, mask, numb and prevent us from seeing deeper existential or spiritual holes. Lovingly be aware of the ego activity of negative emotions. Who are you before negative emotions? After negative emotions? Who are you now? Allow awareness to see the ego activity of negative emotions."

Round six: An ode to my dear Aunt Tilly—Indulgent Talking:

"Rambling, storytelling, exaggeration, dramatization, repetition, veering way off topic, getting lost in minutia, not taking social cues, talking without listening, controlling, demanding, sucking energy and more. See the element of ego which seeks fulfillment through indulgent talking. We've all been here before: The person with whom you are talking is not listening, not paying attention and is chattering on and on. This is indulgent talking. Nine times out of ten, indulgent talking is burying or numbing hidden pain, old unconscious wounds or a deeply unheard and unseen heart. Lovingly be aware of the ego activity of indulgent talking. Who are you before indulgent talking? After indulgent talking? Who are you now? Allow awareness to see the ego activity of indulgent talking."

Round seven: Yeah, um...Listen, are you gonna have those TPS reports for us this afternoon? Practical Talking:

"Small talk, deep conversation, normal conversation, directions, help, assistance, guidance, joking, storytelling, reminiscing, touching base, just saying hi and more. See the element of ego which seeks fulfillment through practical

262

talking. We all have to communicate and talk, but ego is always present, even in day-to- day normal talking. Ego is always seeking, longing, wanting and needing. Lovingly be aware of the ego activity of practical talking. Who are you before practical talking? After practical talking? Who are you now? Allow awareness to see the ego activity of practical talking."

Round eight: A penny for your thoughts. Thoughts and thinking.

"Okay folks...last one, and then I'll stop pounding on you."

J. looks around the room. You are wiped, but somehow still alert and aware.

"This one is probably the toughest and trickiest."

"Okay. Here it is...no holds barred: Every single thought you've ever had, will ever have in the future and/or are currently having is infiltrated by ego. *Every single thought. All of them.* Allow awareness to see and notice all thoughts...high or low, good or bad, dull or amazing, banal or insightful. Your brain is a chronic thought-processing me, me, me-machine that never stops. All you can do is become *aware* of these thoughts. Do this and most thoughts lose their umph, bite or toxic quality. Lovingly be aware of the ego activity of thoughts and thinking. Who are you before thinking? After thinking? Who are you now? Allow awareness to see the ego activity of thoughts and thinking."

J. takes a big breath and then looks around the room.

"Thank you so much, everyone. I know that was lengthy, but you'll be surprised by the long term, ongoing, unfolding healing effects this mediation-discourse can have. To see ego internally is to unite with your truest self."

J. continues to look around. He looks directly at you: "Welcome back, Badass."

Spiritual Badass Lesson:

Maybe you're beginning to see the big picture here: *Everything* is ego and to become a spiritual badass, *everything* must be held and seen by awareness. There is no perfecting this art. You will slip. You will fall. You will bypass. And you will get up again. You will wake up from the bypass. You will get unstuck. You will move on.

Sometimes it requires an ass whipping to wake you up from a bypass. Sometimes life keeps handing you lemons until, one day, you finally decide to make lemonade. A few lemons here and there are okay. Just don't make a career out of that lemonade stand. I mean—shit, do the math. There is just no way you are going to pay your rent or mortgage with a fifty-cent paper cup of squeezed fruit, water and sugar.

Who are you before lemonade? After lemonade? Who are you now?

Wake up Badass!

CHAPTER 24
GARBAGE & THE GODDESS

How to handle earthquakes in public places

It's the next day and you are seated in the dining hall eating breakfast. After the meditation last night, there was a small bathroom and tea break before the post-meditation discussion. George and Carolyn politely exited before the discussion and you took the opportunity to join them. Exhausted, you walked back to the dorm, got under the covers and immediately fell asleep.

You half-heartedly stir your oatmeal and stare at your eggs.

Well, at least the coffee is good, you think.

J. walks in with Lenny wrapped around his neck. He sits down at your table after getting himself a cup of coffee. He also has a small plate with a large strawberry on it. He places Lenny and the strawberry plate on the table. Lenny goes to town.

Please don't say it. I'm not in the mood.

"Good Morning, Sunshine."

Arrrgh.

"You are...consistent. Morning," you mutter.

"Yes, I am."

You fiddle with your oatmeal some more while watching Lenny. You reach out and scratch his back. He ignores you. You're no competition for a strawberry.

"It's all garbage," you offer.

"What?" J. replies. "The breakfast? I can get them to..."

"No...everything. Breakfast, Lenny, you, this table, this dining hall, Seven Dragons, your jeep, fly-fishing, the beach, ice cream ... all of it...everything coming out of my mouth. Garbage."

"Aha," J. half-nods. "You've been thinking."

"Oh, I've been thinking," you retort. *"I've been thinking it's all shit...life, the world, the pizza delivery guy. I mean, how could I not think that after yesterday's little wisdom teaching? I didn't ask to see ego—outside, inside or on the back of a cereal box.*

But now I've seen it and, fuck me, it's just all shit and garbage."

"You done?" asks J.

"Yep."

"You are correct, but you are also *not* correct."

"Well, that is good news. Please...please explain to me how I— am—not—correct."

J. takes a long slow sip of his coffee.

"Well, if viewed only from ego...yeah, it all can very easily appear as...garbage. It's the reason so many people are depressed. Right? I mean, who wouldn't be depressed in this dark world without some glimmer of hope or light? It would be absolutely horrid."

"But you are wrong, you see...because *you* have a glimmer; *you* have hope. It's just not shining as brightly and steadily as you'd like it to right now, and it doesn't help that yesterday I turned off all your ego-made artificial lights.

"Are you following me? This is big grown-up stuff here. Big grown-up stuff doesn't come along without pushing the small kid stuff out of the way.

"Big stuff. Big stuff? Awareness, I suppose?" You only slightly try to hide the undercurrent of your irritation and fatigue.

"Yes, but bigger and steadier than you've tasted it. Right now, you're in the birth canal. Sometimes you see the light and sometimes you don't. I remember when I went through all this shit...it was like being tossed around in a washing machine."

"That's for sure."

J. scratches Lenny on the back. "You good?"

"I'm...okay."

"I'm going into town today with Tenzin. He has a doctor's appointment. I'm driving him. Why don't you join us? We'll hit an art gallery or something while he's at his appointment."

You nod in approval.

"Sounds good."

"I'm hungry. I'm having what *he's* having. Watch him for a minute, will you? Lenny, behave!"

J. gets up from the table and walks over to the breakfast bar.

"Lenny...you're not garbage."

Lenny looks at you, bobs his head up and down and then continues to munch slowly on his big strawberry.

I swear to God that lizard knows what I'm saying.

The name of this chapter was inspired by the title of a book written by Franklin Jones (1939-2008), a former teacher of mine.

Garbage and the Goddess was published in 1974 and is now out of print. Like most of his books, *Garbage and the Goddess* is a great read if you're careful to separate the wheat from the chaff. "Goddess" was his spiritual term for manifest existence...aka everything. And "garbage" was the adjective he used to describe *everything* the Goddess had to offer. He, too, saw existence bereft of awareness, consciousness, light—whatever you want to call it—as a pretty dismal affair. But, *with* light, to quote another book title of his, "Humor Suddenly Returns."

I'm not going to quote any of his stuff here, because his organization is pretty anal about such things, but I will comment on his style. He was one of the first teachers to use the "crazy wisdom" style of teaching, which (if it hasn't dawned on you) is also my preferred teaching M.O.

Franklin later changed his name about half a dozen times before settling on *Adi Da* and his teaching style morphed into a big, fat, cultic, guru-worshipping mess. But for a sweet short time, Franklin was down-to-earth, funny and relatable. I never met Franklin but I did meet Adi Da. *Sigh...*

I'm mentioning this because I think the world and society has changed since those days. *Married with Children, The*

Simpsons, South Park, The Office, Breaking Bad, Fight Club, Fleabag and all the *Marvel Movies* are just a few pop-culture examples of how modern society has embraced dealing with shadow. We now tend to wear our shadows more openly, on our sleeves and with more light-hearted humor.

"Crazy wisdom" teachers like Franklin Jones, Chogyam Trungpa, Jiddu Krishnamurti, G. I. Gurdjieff and, more recently, Jed McKenna have always been the rare endangered species of teachers. I understand the reasons for this unicorn status: ethically and morally "crazy wisdom" can be a slippery slope.

But the slope can be slippery for all the overly serious, dry- as-fuck, new-age or Indian guru types as well. More than one of these guys has gone down in spectacular scandal-ridden flames. Bhagwan Shree Rajneesh (Osho), anyone? To each his own, I suppose. To round out my diatribe, here's my point:

I think if you're going to destroy a person's ego, expose all of its garbage and make them go through dark-night-of-the-soul hell, you sure as fuck should do them the courtesy of demonstrating what lies on the other side of that destruction with a little humor, charm, art and happiness.

In other words, practice what you preach.

A little after noon you, Tenzin and J. all pile into the Jeep. J. drives. It's a circuitous and windy road down the mountain into Asheville. J. and Tenzin reminisce and chit-chat most of the way. You and Lenny are comfortable zoning out in the back seat. His usual perch branch has been moved to the far back and he's enjoying a back scratch facilitated by your thumb and index finger.

You arrive at the center of downtown. It's a busy, artsy, fun little city with lots of people milling around. There are quite a few musical buskers and a gaggle of skater punks on one corner; a skinny mime has even set up shop outside a busy restaurant. It's a sunny day. Asheville is hoppin'.

J. finds a parking space and the three of you get out. Tenzin places a few quarters in the parking meter. Lenny happily takes his place on J.'s shoulders.

J. looks to Tenzin and asks, "How long is your appointment today?"

"I don't know for sure. Probably an hour or two. Depends on how much time Brent has."

"Got it. We're headed to Woolworth's. Gonna check out some art; maybe get a malted milkshake. Meet you at Doc's in about an hour?"

"Sounds great." Tenzin agrees affably and walks off toward his appointment.

"Is Tenzin okay?" you ask J.

"He's fine. Just a regular visit. Brent is great. You'll like his place."

Brent? These guys are on a first name basis with a doctor?

You find this a little odd but blow it off.

You head off with J. and Lenny towards *Woolworth Walk*, an old Woolworth's Five and Dime store converted a few decades ago into a spacious open art gallery—home to about one hundred fifty local artists.

In route, Lenny gets his usual fare of fawning and smartphone selfie requests. J. is loving every minute of it.

Have lizard, become rock star, you muse.

You arrive at *Woolworth Walk* and enter. It's filled with rows of gallery booths, each housing a single artist. At a glance you can see painters, potters, woodworkers, weavers, jewelers, photographers, glass blowers, metalsmiths and more. It's a cornucopia of creative sight and sound.

"Shall we?" asks J.

You commence wandering down an aisle.

"I brought you here for a reason."

"Figured that," you reply.

"Here…," J. gestures widely with both arms to the entire facility, "…is the answer to your comment this morning about everything being garbage. As you can see—it is not. Life bereft of awareness—well yes, I would have to agree with you—is kinda garbage. But with awareness…," he gestures again to the entire room, "…you get this."

"So you're saying that destroying my whole life and every last thing in it is okay because there's—eh, art?"

"No dumb-butt. I'm saying there's *awareness*. Dismantle ego and the only thing left is awareness—the *source* of art and humor and creativity and joy and love and puppy dogs and rainbows. You know…good shit, not garbage.

"I can't tell if you're being serious or not."

"Okay, I went overboard with puppy dogs and rainbows, but when ego gets out of the way, a lot of good things actually do swoop in to take its place. Well, no—actually, I take that back— just *one good thing* swoops in and it's not really a thing, it's the absence of a...doesn't really matter. "

J. pauses to adjust Lenny and then takes a deep breath.

"I know it seems like the end of the world when the lights go down on your whole ego world, identity and project. But what you will find is that those artificial ego lights get replaced by the big, beautiful natural light of the sun. You just gotta give it time."

J. pauses.

"It's hard not to speak in metaphors. Awareness is all I'm talking about—not garbage at all. Hell, awareness is the source of *Star Wars* and the Force. Need I say more?"

"That was a pretty rousing speech."

"Thank you. I practiced that one a lot. Did you like my puppy dogs and rainbows ad lib?"

"Nope."

"Darn it...the *Star Wars Force* one?"

"Better."

"I'll take that. You wanna get a milkshake?"

"Here?" You look at J.

"Yeah, in the back. It's awesome. They've recreated a 1950s soda fountain counter in the back. You can even get lunch there."

You head to the soda fountain, sit down and order sandwiches and shakes. After your food arrives, you have a few bites and, feeling better, you're able to collect your thoughts.

You turn to J. and comment.

"Awareness...art, love...I get it. But you have to remember—all this stuff is old hand to you and brand-spanking-new to me. The positive benefits of awareness are probably abundant and perfectly obvious to you. But I'm just now figuring out what awareness even is. So, when you say that it's freeing and great and awesome—well, I have felt some glimpses of that, but nothing compared to what you and Tenzin have probably experienced. You feel me?"

J. looks at you with a respect, admiration and charm that somehow seems new to you.

"If we weren't in public, I think I'd give you a hug," he says, and then continues. "I feel you. That was very well said. That's how you do it. You own it and you're in charge. You'll have to settle for a fist bump. Or better yet..."

J. clanks his milkshake against yours and you both smile at the unspoken mutually agreed upon milestone of truth-telling... ownership equality.

Inside, you are grinning ear to ear.

You walk out of Woolworth's light as air and more infected with awareness than you had realized. Each step you take is slow and methodical.

Oh shit, I'm Zen Lenny right now! This is the 'awareness now' moment again!! Okay. Yes. This is very cool.

The walk to the Jeep is a delightful series of near-perfect *now* moments. You are on fire with the bliss of the moment. Once there, J. deposits a few more coins in the meter and gestures for you to follow him. You walk two more blocks and round the corner.

"Here we are."

You look up and what you read makes you laugh and groan at the same time.

"Are you shitting me!?" you blurt out.

"Nope—welcome to *Dr. Feel Good's Tattoos.*"

"He was getting a tattoo! Oh, man..."

"Not just *any* tattoo," J. interrupts. "He's been working on it for quite a few months. Come on; wait 'til you see it."

You enter *Dr. Feel Good's* with J. and are surprised at how clean, well-lit, neat and orderly the place is. There are several Japanese six panel room dividers stationed about for privacy. Tattoo-themed artwork and photographs of tattoos cover the walls. You can hear the buzzing, humming and rubbing sound of a tattoo machine behind one of the room dividers.

"We're over here!" someone exclaims.

You and J. walk toward the buzzing going on behind the nearest panel. You round the panel to see Tenzin lying-prostrate on a padded table. He's mostly covered with a white sheet and you can't really make out the tattoo. Seated next to him is a big man, probably the better of 250 pounds and in his mid-forties; he chuckles when he sees the three of you.

"J., Lenny!!! Good to see you!"

"Hey, man. How goes it?!" responds J, with sincere enthusiasm.

J. turns to you. "Brent, this is my friend."

"Pleased to meet you."

"Likewise," you reply.

"Gimme a sec." Brent concentrates on the tattoo tool and Tenzin's shoulder. "Has your friend seen it?"

Tenzin speaks, face still down. "I don't think so."

"There we go. Done that part!" exclaims Brent. He then turns off the tattoo machine and he pulls back the white sheet. "Viola..!"

"Holy crap," you squeak out, astounded.

"Wow, it's progressed," says J. "Just gorgeous."

Covering Tenzin's entire back and upper shoulder region is the most magnificent intricate, multi-colored Chinese dragon you have ever seen. It's every bit the tattoo equal of the seven dragon statues in the meditation hall. The same composed tranquil equanimity married to a fierce, confident, deadly, *do-not-fuck-with-me* vibe. It's perfect eye candy. Tenzin's muscular upper body adds nicely to the effect.

277

"Damn, that is some elegantly fierce art," you compliment both Brent and Tenzin.

"Thanks. Indeed, it is. No easy task." says Brent. "You can sit up now." He taps Tenzin on the shoulder.

Tenzin sits up and turns toward you. Just then, you notice *another* much smaller tattoo on his right upper chest...and that's when...your day turns completely upside down.

The smaller tattoo is unquestionably a phoenix...the *same* type of fiery red phoenix your deceased Uncle Sam had on *his* right upper chest. Your reaction to seeing the tattoo is near instantaneous and cancels out any intrigue created by the coincidence.

You buckle over as your stomach tightens and your lips quiver. Your heart, clenched in a vise, gives way to heaving tears. You are shocked and embarrassed, but can do nothing to hold it back.

"Oh, man, oops. What did I do now?" you hear J. exclaim.

"Uncle Sssss- sssss-aaa...," you continue crying, unable to articulate, and point to the tattoo on Tenzin's chest.

Tenzin looks at you and surmises: "Your Uncle Sam had one of these."

You manage a *"yeah"* through the tears.

You collapse to the ground, astounded at your inability to hold any of this back.

Brent speaks: "Hey guys, let's go to my office. I have a couch and I can get your friend here a cup of water."

J. leans over and gently helps you up.

Brent places a big hand on your shoulder and offers "Maybe we can work this through right now if you're willing."

You look up and see that Brent is directing this offer to you. You nod hesitantly but affirmatively.

Tenzin gets up from the massage table and puts on a t-shirt; Brent stands up and, joining the other two, helps you walk into the back office while you continue to heave and sob.

"Oh, shit. What a mess." You can only squeak and try to laugh.

"It's alright. It's time," J. assures you.

Brent looks to J. and asks "Your friend? ...working on I-issues or We-issues?"

"Mostly I-issues."

"Cool," says Brent. "That'll help."

As you sit down on the couch in Brent's office, J. looks at you and says, "Well, you've come to the right place to do this. Brent, here, used to be a psychotherapist."

Okay, quick break.

You didn't think I'd let you go straight into a therapy session without some sort of commentary or setup, did you? You know me better than that by now.

Okay. I'll try to make this brief. Here we go:

Psychotherapy and the problems inherent in society and the modern-day family can basically be boiled down to two things:

I-issues and We-issues. They are not separate and do not exist independently.

Here's how they operate together: To have a strong healthy independent sense of "I," you need to have been brought up or nurtured in the context of a strong, healthy "We" (family, friends, school, neighborhood, social setting). However, most "We" situations are flawed at best, dysfunctional at worst and just plain dangerous if really bad. The better your nurture/nature upbringing in the "We," usually the better your "I."

As far as society in general is concerned...well, I think it's pretty obvious. We aren't living in an enlightened utopia. We live in a society filled with perpetual cycles of "I-We" poverty. Our grandparents were fucked up. The bad "We" of our grandparents caused both our parents to have bad "I's". Our bad "I" parents formed a "We" and brought us into the world. You and I are now being parented by two individuals with a bad sense of "I" and a marginally held together sense of "We."

And on and on it goes…

We're all lucky to escape this bullshit circus of I-issues and We-issues. So, now enter Freud and Jung and psychotherapy trying to figure all this shit out, of course from the *I* and *We* point of view. The problem with trying to fix I and We from the point of view of I and We is that it's a closed system. As Einstein once famously said, *"We cannot solve our problems with the same thinking we used when we created them."* So, while psychotherapy may be able to solve *some* of the I-We issues, it can never fully solve them all.

For full healing and true growth to occur, we need an intervention by something *outside* of the "I-We" dynamic. We need something that precedes or transcends all the I-issues and

We-issues. That something is *awareness.* Now...enter spirituality.

Okay, I'm arriving at my point here:

As you may have noticed, the spiritual badass process of inviting awareness into the middle of the "I-We" dynamic is to invite the de-facto end of the usual "I-We." Awareness dismantles the whole identity ego project and takes over. "I" gets shattered. "We" gets shattered.

This whole process sounds dramatic, I know– but it isn't. Simply put, awareness becomes dominant, allowing for true healing to take place.

Here's the deal though: You just can't willy-nilly decide to end the *I-We* dynamic. You can't merely abandon it. You can't bypass it. You can't ignore it. "I" needs to be healed. "We" needs to be healed. There's just no getting around it. Your "I-We" issues aren't going away without a fight.

When we start fucking around with spiritual badass awareness, our "I-We" issues are going to come barreling up. As you're about to find out, however, the *I-We* healing process that's facilitated through spiritual badass awareness is a lot simpler and quicker than you'd think.

Oh and—to all you psychotherapists out there—One: What the fuck are you doing reading this book in the first place? And Two: I am fully aware that this is a crude, albeit apropos, description of your livelihood. If it bothers you, *call me.* I will gladly provide counseling at my regular $600 an hour rate. It may take us years, however, to get to the bottom of this debacle.

Break over.

While Brent is a very large man with scary tattoos up and down his arms and a goatee to match, you look into his eyes and recognize that he's also a very gentle man. He's a big teddy bear. This recognition disarms and relaxes you and, to a certain degree, quells your sobbing.

You sit down on the couch. J. takes a seat beside you. Tenzin brings you a cup of water and then sits crossed leg and relaxed on the floor against a nearby wall. Brent grabs a small pillow and throws it to Tenzin. Tenzin places it between his back and the wall. Brent grabs his big, black, leather rolling office chair and drags it over in front of the sofa. J. pulls a few treats out of his pocket and sets Lenny on the ground with them.

Everyone settles.

Your mind is continually drawn back to your uncle. Each time it returns to him, you heave—hunched over, elbows on knees, hands in your face. Your eyes are wet, puffy and red. Your heart hurts. Your stomach is as tight as an outer steel hatch on a submarine.

Brent gazes at you with sympathy.

"So, I'll share and then you share... okay?"

You nod affirmatively.

"J. is right. I used to be a therapist. I'm no longer practicing, mainly because I realized I wanted to be an artist, so this is more like advice, okay?"

Somehow you feel that this is going to be more than advice.

"Yeah," you respond.

"Also...apologies. I don't have a lot of time. My next tattoo client is in about an hour. So this will have to be quick and dirty, alright? But this should be okay if you've been working on your *I* stuff."

Brent looks to J. and asks, "Mindfulness, presence-awareness, ego—good grasp?"

J. replies: "Yeah, pretty good."

J. then looks at you and says, "Remember *two yeses*. Yes to fear. Yes to awareness."

You instinctively take a deep breath and place your attention on your whole body.

Brent continues. "So that's my share. How about you? Why don't you start by telling us about your uncle."

You sit up, rub your eyes, and then take another big breath.

"Okay. Well, um, Uncle Sam. When my Dad left, my Uncle Sam sort of took over. Filled in the...gap."

"How old?" asks Brent.

"I was about eight," you respond. *"My dad was an alcoholic; fought with Mom all the time. Big mess. So, when Dad left...after the divorce, Uncle Sam came around more. I really..."*

You start breaking down again.

"loved...Uncle Sam, but then, God-fucking damn-it. Fucking car crash. Why the fuck? Everything taken. He didn't deserve it. He was wise, kind, funny and then, just fuck you world, fuck you God, fuck this shit."

You wail a bit more and then catch yourself.

"Damn, this is hitting hard. I'm trying...aware. Just..."

"It's all good. There's no perfecting this. Let it be sloppy." Brent comments.

"Thanks."

You pause.

"So that's it, essentially. Uncle Sam died when I was about thirteen. My uncle had the same tattoo....as Tenzin."

Tenzin smiles compassionately at you from his spot on the floor. You chuckle to yourself and look around.

"This is the strangest therapy I've ever had," you comment. Everyone laughs.

"Okay, so let's do this." Brent speaks. "Uncross your legs, place your feet flat on the ground and breathe deeply a few more times."

You do so.

"Place your attention on all the parts of your body. Notice the one who is aware of your body, that empty part doing the noticing. Notice awareness, or as I call it—*presence* itself."

You close your eyes and concentrate.

"This may be a little tricky right now, given that you're a bundle of raw nerves. Do the best you can."

Brent then speaks directly, clearly and concisely.

"Open your eyes and keep eye contact with me. Where does it hurt—right now—in your body?"

"Heart and stomach," you reply without hesitating, then added *"vise grip."*

"Deep breath again. Very good. I want you to allow the wound and pain of the divorce, of your father's absence, and your uncle's death to be fully present. Stop pushing it away. Invite it all the way in...here and now. Allow your heart and stomach to clench all the way. Breathe and be aware while you are doing this."

You try your best. You find it a little difficult to be aware while also being an emotional mess, but somehow it works... a little.

Oh—okay, there it is.

"Are you there?" Brent asks.

"Best I can be," you reply.

"Beautiful. Try to be as present as you can—and allow the pain of that event, of that time, when you were eight, when you were thirteen, to be here *right now*. Welcome it all here."

He pauses, then continues.

"Remember to breathe...keep eye contact."

Brent takes a deep breath. You look into his eyes and sense something vast, gentle, caring.

Brent continues, "Every crappy situation, every painful circumstance...has *two* sides. Every wound has both a pain *and* a gift."

"The separation of your parents and the absence of your father no doubt created a cocktail of abandonment, unlove, distrust and anti-authority issues. But with it came a gift of fierce independence, perseverance and fortitude."

He pauses and maintains eye contact with you.

"We're not trying to fix or change your past. But we can find that eight-year-old who is—believe it or not, still with you as this wound in your heart and stomach—and with awareness or presence, acknowledge the eight-year-old, see the eight-old-year old, thank the eight-year-old, hold the eight-year-old, love the eight-year-old and let that little person go. Can you do this?"

He pauses again. You take a big breath and nod.

"That little person did the best he could. That little person made you who you are today."

You return to being a watery mess as you tacitly feel the pain of your eight-year-old self.

"Breath and be aware. You're doing great."

You nod and then rub your eyes. Tenzin gets up, hands you a tissue, and then sits back down. You notice the same intense clear eye contact in both Tenzin and J.

They're here—down here...in here...with me, you think appreciatively.

Brent continues.

"Okay. Halfway there. Once again...remember to breathe. Keep eye contact. Don't push the pain away. Welcome it. Be present to it."

He pauses.

"Every crappy situation, every painful circumstance...has two sides. Every wound has a pain and a gift. Your uncle was kind, gentle, wise and funny—everything you needed at that time. The wound of your uncle's death was, no doubt, a great one. This wound caused a deep distrust in all things pertaining to meaning and purpose. His death so random and meaningless...Fuck you, God and life—right?"

He breathes and pauses.

"The gift in the death of your uncle was the development in you of kindness, an open mind, an open heart...without being gullible, flaky or easily swayed. His death gave you a beautifully balanced sense of integrity, skepticism and street smarts—all of which have served you well."

Another pause.

You notice the return of the same deep, heavy, open-eyed meditating experience you've recently had.

The sobering truth. Here it is again. This is also the sobering truth!

Brent continues, "So, we can't fix or change this part of your past either. But we can find that thirteen-year-old who is still with you right now in the form of this deep wound in your heart and stomach—and we can do for that person what we did for the eight-year-old...

Acknowledge, see, thank, hold and love that young person. And then, let that young person go. That very young person also did the best he could. That very young person made you who you are today."

You heave, sigh, cry a little more and then—you relax deeply into the moment, into the depth of your own skin and blood and bones…and into an intense present awareness.

You are dizzy, exhausted, vulnerable and yet, utterly light, still and free.

Damn, you think to yourself. A few minutes pass in silence.

Eventually, and oddly, all you can think about is eating a hotdog and drinking a Coke at Woolworths.

"I'm hungry," you comment.

Brent laughs. "Your blood sugar is low. Eh, hold on…I have a Coke in the fridge."

Brent stands and leaves the room.

Tenzin gets up and walks over to you. "You need another one of these?" he asks, offering another tissue.

"Thanks," you reply, taking it. You dry your eyes with it and then blow your nose.

J. pats you on the back. "Well done," he says.

"Thanks, guys." You glance gratefully at Tenzin and J.

Brent returns and hands you a glass of Coke with ice. You gulp it down.

Brent looks you directly in the eyes and says, "You've done some good work with these guys…I can tell. Your eyes are very clear, very present. Don't let them pester you any more for a while, though. Go home and get some rest. It may take some time for all this to sink in."

"Roger that," you reply.

Tenzin pats Brent on the back. J. picks Lenny off the floor, then drapes him gently across his shoulder. J. then offers his hand to Brent and they shake.

"Brent, you're a true artist."

"Thanks," replies Brent.

"You are...truly gifted." you comment and then, because it seems absolutely appropriate, you bow, just as the *Seven Dragons* monks would do, with your hands at your heart. Brent returns the bow.

"We're all in this together," he says with a smile.

The four of you walk over to the exit door of *Dr. Feel Good's Tattoo* shop.

"Be well, friends!" Brent exclaims and then heads back into his shop.

Tenzin, J. and you walk in silence back to the Jeep, Lenny perched on J.'s shoulder. Lenny seems to understand the importance of not drawing the usual attention and strikes his napping pose.

Once inside the Jeep, J. asks, "Did you want to get something to eat?"

"Actually...I'm good. I can wait until we get back to the sanctuary."

"Cool." J. puts the Jeep in drive and commences the return journey.

In the back seat again, you close your eyes thinking that today's chapter is over.

Except—it isn't.

You probably should have eaten something.

Halfway through the drive, on the twisty, uphill part of the road...it hits.

Not sadness. Not grief. Not loss. And not anything to do with any *I* or *We* that you can think of.

It's the return of the horror, dread and fear of your imminent demise—the same awful horror show you first felt at Mt. Vesuvius Mini Golf Park.

Oh God. Oh, God. Oh—God! Not again! You think. You squirm and scramble for an escape—but there is none. The panic attack overtakes you. All you can do is watch and witness...

Right! Oh God. Say yes to fear; yes to awareness. Yes to...

The panic attack gets stronger and stronger. You refuse to vocalize it, not wanting to drag Tenzin and J. into your personal hell for a second time today.

Fuck this shit! No. NO. NO! NO!!

You breathe and keep repeating defiantly.

No! NO! NO!! Not now. Go away. Not now. Go away. Not now—go away!

It works...eventually.

Slowly, the panic attack recedes. By the time you return to the sanctuary, you're an exhausted limp rag. J. parks the Jeep and all three of you get out. J. fist bumps Tenzin.

Tenzin bows to you, smiles and, as he's walking away, says "See you in an hour or so."

"Sounds good," J. calls out to Tenzin.

J. turns to you.

"We're heading to the drop before dinner. You wanna join?"

"Oh, fucking God— no," you reply.

"Totally understand." replies J.

"You gonna be okay on your own for a while?"

"I'll be fine. I'm gonna lie down."

"Cool. You know where to find me."

You sigh with relief as you enter your little dorm room. Now, at last, you think to yourself, this chapter…this day is over. *Holy shit…this was a long one.* You then drift off into a long sleep.

Spiritual Badass Lesson:

Someday when you're ready or when it's your time...reread this chapter. If it provides even a smidgeon of clarity as your journey down this glorious, crazy, tumultuous path unfolds, then I've done my job.

And if that time is now—and you are here for a second look—congratulations and well done, my friend. Well done.

CHAPTER 25
CAROWINDS

How to meet ultimate fear

The next day you wake up super early, because—*oops!* You fell asleep around 6pm the previous night, skipped dinner and slept for twelve hours.

You probably would have slept even longer had it not been for the faint rustling sound from the piece of paper that was just placed under your door.

You get up, stretch and shuffle over to the door and lean down. You pick up the stationery with the official *Seven Dragons Sanctuary* logo on it.

It reads:

-Day of Silence-

Just a gentle reminder: Friday is our traditional Day of Silence. We do this as a way to strengthen and seal the benefits of your stay at our sanctuary and to prepare you for your departure home or to Carowinds on Saturday.

Remembering that you and J. were last minute drop-in guests of Tenzin, you place the piece of paper in your pocket as a reminder to maintain silence.

Well, this should be interesting, you muse.

Either that, or I'll go bat-shit crazy.

Oh God! Really? I have to listen to my thoughts all day? Fuuuuuuuck.

Carowinds?

I wonder what that is?

You get dressed and then meander over to the dining hall to grab a coffee.

Well, this is awkward.

There aren't many people up or in the dining hall yet but the few that are also observe the Day of Silence. You nod to George and Carolyn and a monk who's also up early before getting your coffee.

You sit alone at a table and sip on your coffee wondering what to do. You start to get anxious.

You notice your mind is, indeed, going a little bat-shit crazy. One of its favorite, expected, daily and utterly routine pastimes has just been yanked away.

No talking, no complaining, no chit-chatting, no laughing, no deep conversation, no frivolous bantering, no, no, no...

The caffeine doesn't help either. You notice its effect on your mind. Normally the caffeine would get channeled straight through your big fat mouth—but now it's log-jammed in your head.

Oh, boy...

More people walk into the dining hall and you nod to them as well.

Your anxiety goes up another notch. Now you see it. It's not the silence…

I'm exposed! They can see me—no personality talking head filters—just the empty, bland, nothing...me.

And then, another insight:

Oh shit, we're...all...exposed.

We're all empty, nothing...nobodies. All...internal, empty, me.

All naked.

You relax, let go and expand. You fall into the exposure, the vulnerability, the pure nakedness of the experience.

Fuck it. Here I am...nobody special.

Immediately, your anxiety quells.

Jesus Christ—all this just from fucking silence. Who knew!?

You take a few deep breaths and drop into the moment. Nothing to do.

Nothing to say.

Nowhere to go.

Nobody to be.

Nobody to impress.

J. walks in with Lenny wrapped around his neck.

He putters around at the coffee area, then plops himself down across the table from you. You give him a big genuine smile and then an idea pops into your head. You get up, walk across the room, grab a pen and return. You pull out the piece of paper from your pocket and scribble something on the back of it.

You push the paper towards J. It reads:

"Good Morning, Sunshine!

J. laughs out loud and then bows silently to you, grinning from ear to ear. You grab the paper back again and write something else on it:

"Headed to Angel Falls." You show it to J.

He gives you a thumbs up. You smile again and return the bow of silence. Before leaving, you give Lenny a scratch on his head. Preoccupied with a piece of pineapple, Lenny hardly notices.

You take a big breath and walk out—slowly, deliberately and on fire with the vulnerable awareness of being a big fat nobody.

Zen Lenny, you think.

Zen Lenny.

Knock. Knock.

This is a good time to talk about two things: boredom and silence. Spiritual Badasses are friends with both.

Let's start with boredom:

What I have to say about boredom falls into the counterintuitive, uncomfortable truth, anti-advice category.

Do you ever find yourself bored out of your ass? Good.

I am a master at being bored. Being a spiritual badass has that effect. As a matter of fact, most days (even busy days) I always have time for boredom. I'm bored right now, even though I've got plenty of shit to do. I was bored yesterday at 3:04 pm.

Today at 6:37, I'll probably be...bored.

But! I'm totally okay with boredom. I accept it. I allow it. I'm friends with it. I love it. I even relish it.

Normally most of us do everything we can to avoid the awkwardness of *just simply being*. When left alone to our own devices, without some activity or project or entertainment—we become restless, nervous or anxious. We judge ourselves: Oh, I should be doing this or that or the other thing. I should be constructive, helpful, busy, productive, essential, etc. I must do something! I need to be doing...something! Always on the move....always busy...always, always, always...some-*fucking-*thing. Absolutely relentless.

Well, how 'bout this?

Just be fucking bored. Allow yourself to drop completely into boredom...into the anxiety, nervousness, restlessness and/or agitation of that boredom. Fuck it. Stop struggling against it. Why not accept it one hundred percent? Sit your ass down on the sofa and just be fucking bored. I mean what's the worst that can happen? (That's a rhetorical question.)

Answer: You'll finally get a break from the relentless, maniacal task master of mind/ego and settle into the outer periphery of something utterly magical, peaceful and amazing...your own empty, free, spacious aware badass self.

BUT—you gotta go through boredom to get there.

So, next time you're feeling bored..? Good. You're headed in the right direction. Stay with it, endure it, watch it and see how it slowly evaporates and changes. And then, after a while, take a big breath...and from this deliciously free bored space...you can decide what to do next.

Okay, now let's talk about silence:

The first time I ever did a silent retreat—a week of zip—zero—nada—talking, it revolutionized my idea of what a true retreat or vacation was. If you've never done it, you cannot imagine what a profound experience not gabbing for a week is like and what it can do for you. Most people have no clue just how much excess energy leaks out of their pie holes.

At first, maintaining silence is excruciatingly difficult, anxiety inducing and nearly impossible. You will come up with all sorts of ways to cheat.

But, if you stick with it, you will notice yourself slowly sinking into unimaginable depths of awareness and being. It becomes *an utter delight.*

Of course, it can also be an utter nightmare, which is why it's always best to practice silence *after* you've worked on your own internal stuff at least a little. This way you won't be solo fighting, grappling and, most likely, losing to all the demons that pop up.

Silence is this way: For the badass aware you, it's the source of freedom and peace; for the ego-mind-personality you, it's the source of anxiety and fear.

I once did a silent retreat with a teacher and ten other people while canoeing down the Green River in Canyonlands National Park, Utah. I'd worked on my own internal *I-issues* quite a bit by this time, and so, not being one to shy away from spiritual badass excess, I also dropped (liquid, bottle, dropper, under the tongue) a natural psychoactive hallucinogenic drug called salvia divinorum, derived from a Mexican sage plant.

Again, I was an old pro at plumbing internal depths at this point, so the combination of silence and salvia was mind-fucking-blowing amazing. Imagine two-hundred-foot high swirling red-brown rock cliff walls, an unending river, zero light pollution exposing the Milky Way Galaxy in all its glory each night and huge epic southwestern vistas each day. All of it couched, held and viewed through the lens of a salvia-enhanced awareness, stillness and...silence. I wouldn't recommend this combination to everyone (especially beginners), but I do recommend trying a day or two of silence—or more if you can swing it. After the silence kicks your ass and you give in to it a little, you will be amazed.

In short, shutting the fuck up every once in a while will do you a world of good.

You head over to the narrow, wooded entrance path that leads to *Angel Falls*. It's still early, so when you step into the forest, the morning bird symphony is at high volume.

What a gorgeous sound...

The sacredness of the woods and path overtakes you. As you walk, you slowly drop into Zen Lenny movement. Each step is delicate, aware and delightful. Your whole body becomes relaxed, open and fully alive. Your breathing slows...

Oh, this is so awesome.

You notice groups of delicate, chartreuse colored ferns displaying Fibonacci spirals. On a pile of old worn rocks is a deep rich green moss, painted on like old gold patina on antique furniture. Small saplings make futile efforts to reach the daylight canopy hundreds of feet up. A small mocha colored rabbit darts out of nowhere onto the path and, when he notices you, just as quickly jumps back into the undergrowth...

True...church.

You continue walking slowly, with no agenda or deadline— each moment rich with life, flavor, color, sound and an intimacy so ripe and tender you long to dissolve into the forest surroundings forever.

Oddly, what you experience more than anything is *gratitude*. Gratitude for the moment, the deep forest and your good fortune to be here now experiencing it in such a sacred way.

Never before have you experienced such *genuine* gratitude.

So strange...

You notice this gratitude isn't coming from your intellect, or your mind or your head. It's coming from some deep, long forgotten, internal recess of your very own body, heart and being...as if some prehistoric and ancient native bodily intelligence had just been awakened, recognized and held by the forest itself.

So intimate...

You continue walking until you reach *Angel Falls*. Your reverie continues as the gurgling sound of the falls and creek is added to your experience.

You sit down on the bench and, with eyes wide open, fall further into deep blissful silent stillness...

Holy shit...

You notice that silence isn't empty at all. It is filled with richness and depth and life...

You notice that there is no separation between *you* and the silence...

Awareness...is...silence.

You also notice that there is no separation between the silence, awareness, your body *and*...the forest.

Oh, man...my body...is...the forest.

Then, finally...no more thoughts, no more insights, no more epiphanies...

Just simply sitting on a bench in the woods... Time passes.

Your reverie slowly subsides and you notice the return of usual feeling states and mind stuff...

That was the ocean...

I am the wave...

I am both...

You return to normal, but it doesn't bother you much, because the aftertaste of the oceanic experience you just had clearly and gently sends this message: *I will be back...*

I will be back...

You smile inside, get up from the bench and head back to campus.

The Day of Silence passes without much activity. You meander, stroll and visit various spots around the sanctuary. You drop into the meditation hall, but prefer being outside even though the hall contains its own special beauty.

The day drips by slowly and quietly.

You rest and relax in a way you've never experienced before. lunch... a nap... another stroll... sitting quietly... some reading... dinner ... another visit to the meditation hall... and then, bedtime...

It's a new day, Charlie Brown, and the last day for your stay at *Seven Dragons*. At breakfast, J. shared that you will be taking a field trip with whoever else wants to go to Carowinds.

"Oh right, is that some sort of nature meditation spot or something?"

"Nope," J. replies.

"Another retreat center?"

"Nope...," J. says with a slowly creeping smile.

Uh-oh, here we go, you think.

"Okay I'll bite. What exactly is Carowinds?"

J. sets his coffee down and looks directly at you.

"It's home to *The Fury 325,* of course...America's longest steel roller coaster: 1.25 miles of track, a 190 foot tall barrel turn, speeds up to 95 miles per hour and 3.25 minutes of thrills, guaranteed to transform you into a puddle of limp jello."

"Oh crap," you think.

"We're going to an amusement park for our last day?" you regurgitate.

"Abso-fucking-lutely!" replies J., grinning from ear to ear.

J. asks you to pack your things. You will be driving separately to *Carowinds* and, afterwards, will head out on your next adventure (which of course he doesn't detail).

At 9 a.m., everyone gathers in the parking area to say goodbye and to load into respective vehicles. Tenzin is standing next to four other monks and two twenty-something retreatants, Jay and Austin, whom you met briefly a few days ago. They all load into a *Seven Dragons* van, with Tenzin taking the driver's seat.

Tenzin rolls down the window and says to J. "We'll meet you at the entrance area around eleven. Sound good?"

J. responds with a thumbs up.

"Awesome. See you at *Carowinds.*"

Tenzin pulls out and down the driveway. George and Carolyn are here.

You walk up to them.

"Not going to the park?" you ask.

"Afraid not," says Carolyn.

"Well, it was so nice to meet you; thank you so much for sharing your story this week. I really enjoyed hanging out with you guys."

"Us too," says George. "Be well, friend."

You can't resist a hug and extend one to each of your new friends.

"You really helped me," you add. *'Thank you."*

"You ready?" you hear J. exclaim.

You say goodbye to a few of the monks not going to *Carowinds* and then walk over to the Jeep.

"You want me to drive?" asks J.

"I'm good," you say and grab the keys from J.

You take a peek in the backseat and see Lenny in his usual spot. You hop in and, with a heavy heart, depart the *Seven Dragons Sanctuary.*

Damn … you think to yourself.

What a place…

What an amazing place…

Within a few minutes, you are down the mountain and on Interstate 26 headed south. *Carowinds* is about a two-hour drive.

You settle in for the journey.

In the rearview mirror, you see Lenny dozing off on his favorite branch and you think:

How is Lenny going to fucking ride a roller coaster?

The journey is relatively quick and painless, the GPS on your phone delivering you to the *Carowinds* entrance gate, in Charlotte, North Carolina, shortly after 11 a.m. It's Saturday so the big sprawling parking lot is nearly full. J. had texted Tenzin and you meet at a designated spot. You pull up next to the *Seven Dragons* van.

Tenzin, four other monks, Jay and Austin all get out of the van with big smiles on their faces. You chuckle inside at the sight of five monks, still dressed in their traditional maroon and yellow robes, about to get jiggy with it at an amusement park.

J. takes Lenny out of the Jeep, offering him the usual comfortable shoulder wrap.

"How is that going to work?" you ask J., clearly referring to Lenny's inability to get on rides.

"We'll take turns," J. says.

"Oh—of course," you respond.

The gaggle of *Seven Dragons* fellas trek across the parking lot, wait in line to show entrance passes and then purchase tickets. Within ten minutes you are walking down the main thoroughfare, strolling the streets of *Carowinds*.

The sights, smells and sounds of today's experience stand in stark contrast to yesterday's silent and sacred repose.

This is fucking insanity, you think to yourself.

The sounds of coasters and tracks and joyful screaming and pop music piped in through hidden speakers...

A thousand sights: huge concrete walkways lined with perfect garden landscapes, monster-sized rides painted in primary colors everywhere you look, hundreds of people milling about, small kiosks filled with hotdogs and Coke and popcorn, shooting gallery games with over-sized stuffed animal prizes and caricature artists offering their services...

It's a complete reversal of your recent experience, and deep down inside you can't help but laugh. Your inner laughter soon manifests as an outward smile.

Tenzin sees you smiling and asks, "What'll it be first?"

"NOT a roller coaster!" you immediately respond.

"Okay-doke..." Tenzin says. "How about that one!?"

He points to a ride called "Electro-Spin"—a whirling, spinning, twisting six-armed beast which looks just horrifying.

"Eh—well—"

"Cool. Let's do it." Tenzin leads the way.

You swallow your hesitation and decide it's as good as any, and better than a coaster to start with.

J. hands Lenny to one of the monks who wants to sit this one out and the group of you gets in line. It's a relatively short wait and ten minutes later your amusement park cherry has been popped. You are queasy, jello-legged and dizzy—but smiling from ear to ear. The *Electro-Spin* delivered. You whooped, you hollered, you nearly vomited...and are now ready to tackle the whole park.

The day passes quickly as your normally tranquil and sensible *Seven Dragons* monks, new friends and iguana troop around the park. Rides are conquered. Pictures are taken. Prizes at game booths are won. Lenny is fawned over. The monks are fawned over.

The group of you even scores shortcut line passes to a few of the bigger rides.

It's an awesomely fun day. You aren't thinking about spiritual matters, or awareness or your place in the grand cosmic scope of shit; you're just riding a bunch of big stupid rides and enjoying the crap out of it.

It's around three in the afternoon now and there's one ride the group hasn't been on. Not for a lack of trying, it's just that *The Fury 325* lines were *way* too long. But finally, as luck would have it, the lines look thinned out and you all decide to take advantage.

It's a monster.

The Fury 325 looms three hundred twenty-five feet over you (hence, its namesake) as you wait in its short line. It gives you pants-shitting tremors just looking at it.

There's no way to prevent the fear that just gazing at it induces. The blood-curdling screams of the passengers ahead of you don't help.

You, J., Tenzin, Jay, Austin and three other monks inch slowly toward the boarding platform. Lenny is with the fourth monk waiting on a nearby bench.

Oh shit, oh shit, oh shit...

J. looks at you and senses your fear.

307

"Remember the two yeses," he says.

Oh fuck! Really? I have to do that here!? You resist, but then give in.

Yes to awareness. Yes to fear. Yes to awareness. Yes to fear...

Your group is next to board...

The coaster currently on the tracks drifts off and begins its ascent to the three hundred twenty-five foot peak. You look up, nervous as shit now.

It disappears on the downhill and you hear the screams...

Oh motherfucker....yes to awareness, yes to fear...

The second of the two coasters that rotate on the tracks pulls into the boarding bay. You watch as people with smiles of exuberance and legs of jello stand up to unload.

It empties and your gate bar swings open. Your group fills up the first two rows of the coaster. You take a seat in the very fucking front car of the Beast. Next to you are J., Tenzin and one of the other monks. The waist-level safety harness and handlebar move into position, pinning you hard against the seat.

Oh fuck. Oh, fuck...

There is no denying your raw nerves and fear now.

Remember to breathe. Remember to breathe...

A buzzer goes off and you are given *two* thumbs up by the coaster operator. You roll out.

There is no slow clackity-clack of the coaster going up because this thing is on some kind of motorized track. You zoom to the top in seconds. The height is dizzying. You try not to look around...

You crest the peak.

Yes to awareness...fear...awareness...fear...

You hang slightly over the top edge as the back cars of the roller coaster hinder you from completely releasing.

3-2-1:

Ohhhhhhhhhh —Fuuuuuuuuuuuuuuuuuuuck!!!!

You have only awareness to thank as you drop, weightless at an 81-degree angle, nearly straight down. You can barely breathe. Your body tingles and you are dizzy with the utter rush of the drop. Weirdly enough, you also completely recognize awareness and, because of it, your entire body relaxes.

You reach bottom and pull out into a mighty inverted barrel turn. You watch as your vision tunnels due to the speed, and you nearly black out. You pull out of the barrel roll, your full vision returns, and you allow your body to relax even further.

You speed up another hill. *Relax. Aware.*

Round a sharp corner. *Relax. Aware.*

Whip into another downhill. *Relax. Aware.*

Roll inverted into another barrel. *Relax. Aware. Holy fuuuuuuuuuuuuck! This is incredible!!!!!*

Accept. Relax. Aware. Embrace. Enjoy. No fear...

You suck every last bit of the ride into your being. It's magnificent...utterly freeing and amazing. What at first filled you with complete horror and dread has now morphed into a source of amazing joy and freedom.

You whoop and holler on the last downhill and the coaster swings into the station.

You are exhausted, overwhelmed, and utterly delighted.

You look at J., Tenzin and the other monk. They all have gigantic grins on their faces.

The coaster slowly pulls into the station. The safety harness releases and you stand.

Oh God. Complete Jello—as advertised...

You place a hand on Tenzin's shoulder as you wobble to gain your footing. You quickly regain your balance and walk with the rest of your group down the exit ramp.

You see Lenny astride the fourth monk's shoulder.

"What next!?" Tenzin quizzes the group.

The group huddles and talks, but you opt to wait the next one out and go over to Lenny. You peel him gently off the monk's shoulders and place him over your own. He's happy sitting on anyone's shoulders and quickly makes himself at home.

J. looks toward you and asks, "You sitting this one out?"

"Yeah...need a break. I'll take Lenny. Gonna go get a Coke or something at the Carowinds Café. You guys enjoy."

J. smiles at you and pats Lenny on the head. "Be good," he says to you both. "Meet you there in a bit."

"We'll be fine." You offer J. assurance and watch as the group walks off toward some other ride.

You proceed toward the café with Lenny on your shoulders. Your legs are still goo-ish, shaky jello and it takes a while for them to return to normal. You arrive at the café, enter and order a Coke with ice.

With drink in hand, you head to an upstairs seating area. You climb the steps and discover that the area is completely empty. *Nice*, you think and are aware that you feel grateful for this unexpected treat.

You and Lenny plop down to an empty table that overlooks the large walking plaza outside. You stare vacantly out over the crowds as you sip your Coke. Your eyes land on a t-shirt.

Holy shit! What are the chances? you think.

Another red phoe-

The red phoenix on the t-shirt immediately triggers the memory of your time at *Dr. Feel Good's Tattoo* and the session with Brent. That, in turn, triggers the memory of the brain earthquake on the car ride home. And *that* triggers the earthquake again.

Oh, no. Not now. You try to calm yourself, but it's too late.

The quake rumbles into full intensity in a matter of seconds. Crushing waves of terror wash over your body. You become faint with raw, unmitigated fear.

A part of you knows there is no pushing this anxiety attack away.

But you try—

NO! NO! NO! NO! You whisper. This fails.

The quake gets stronger. You start to sweat. Chills overtake you.

You try taking a sip of your Coke—Nope.

You stand up and pace—Nope.

You try petting Lenny—Nope.

You collapse into the chair again.

There is no stopping this thing now.

You then remember *The Fury 325. Fuck it,* you think. *I'm done running.*

You sit up in your chair and place your gaze on Lenny's steely little lizard eyes and allow it.

You take a big breath.

You are more than scared. You are immobilized with the fear of your own world-ending death. But you have no recourse, no escape plan, no options...

You stare at the lizard.

Awareness is your only recourse.

Awareness is your only ally.

Awareness is your only island.

Awareness is your only option.

You allow yourself to...completely...relax.

In a split second, a massive wave and rush of fear-induced energy washes over your body and explodes like a nuclear bomb on the horizon. The energy washes head to toe, like a tsunami wave on a deserted beach. You watch.

You witness. You are aware.

You relax more. There is a snapping, crackling, popping sound to the energy. The top of your head opens up. Your entire body tingles.

You are *only* awareness. Nothing left.

Your body melts into total nothingness as the fear energy washes over you. It relaxes you like a limp rag.

And then—it's over as soon as it began. You breathe a sigh of relief and collapse.

It was only fear! ...your last thought before falling out of the chair—and passing out on the floor.

I was twenty-nine years old when this happened to me.

I remember very distinctly staring at an electrical outlet (in my small room in the group farmhouse I was renting) when I finally stopped running from the massive, world-ending, fear-inducing earthquake that had been hounding me for years.

It was quite something. It was like shedding a hundred pounds instantly or freeing myself from some ancient ball and chain. It was also over—in minutes.

I hear your thoughts.

Damn, how can I do that?!

My response is two-fold: One—It's usually a slow gradual build-up, like what you've been reading here, that leads to a radical shift. And two—it doesn't happen the same way for all people.

Allow me to proffer this metaphor: The process of awakening awareness and dismantling ego is a little like melting an iceberg. All icebergs are different. Each contains a unique mixture of fissures, cracks and fault lines. Some icebergs melt gradually and slowly, and the melting is hardly noticed. Other icebergs split and crack with huge chunks of ice slamming into the sea in spectacular fashion. There are an infinite number of ways an iceberg can melt.

There are also an infinite number of ways a human being can dismantle ego and awaken to awareness.

One final note about all this: As you are about to find out, this is by no means the end of the process or our adventure. If you are an astute student of esoteric spiritual literature, you will find numerous vague references to *two* locks on the human being relative to "Knowing Thyself."

The first lock has to do with consciousness or awareness. I have found this to be true. The second lock has to do with the heart. I have found this, also, to be quite true.

"Sir. Can you hear me? Sir!"

Someone is speaking to you.

What the fuck! Why is my face on the floor?

"Sir...are you okay?"

Oh shit, I fucking passed out.

"I'm fine. Yeah, good. Sorry. Oh crap. What..."

"Sir. Should I call an ambulance? Did you hurt yourself?"

You notice that it's the same young man from whom you purchased the Coke downstairs.

"I'm fine. I just...must be exhausted."

"Should I call someone, sir? Is that your iguana?"

He points to Lenny, who is seated comfortably on a nearby wall alcove at the top of the stairs.

"Yeah, that's Len—he's mine."

"He scared the crap out of some young woman...she came running downstairs...said there was a wild iguana on the stairs."

"On the stairs? Lenny, did you..?"

"Are you sure there's no one I can call?"

You sit up, fumble around in your pants pocket and pull out your phone. You hand it to him.

"Sure; just hit redial."

The young man takes your phone and pushes a button. You hear the ring.

"Hello?" you hear faintly.

"Uh hi, your friend, um, just passed out in the Carowinds Café."

"Oh shit," you hear faintly. "We'll be right there."

The young man offers you his hand and helps you to your feet. He then gently guides you to your seat again. You notice Lenny still in his spot. You sit.

"Why don't you take a sip of your Coke, sir? Your friends will be here in a minute, I think."

"Okay...thanks, man. I'll be fine."

"Your iguana, sir?"

"Oh, he'll be fine. He's trained. Don't worry about him."

You rest a few more minutes while sipping your Coke. The young man waits with you in awkward silence.

Holy fuck...that was intense! You recall your encounter with absolute fear.

Holy fuck...

Soon you hear the footsteps of a group of people striding up the steps.

J. appears first and immediately walks over to you. "Damn, what happened here?" J. asks.

You look J. squarely in the eyes.

"Earthquake," you reply.

"Big one."

Tenzin walks up the stairs, sees Lenny and gently places him on his shoulders.

"Everything okay?" he asks.

Jay, Austin and the rest of the monks follow. "I think so," say J.

"I'm fine."

You smile and take another sip of your Coke. For the first time you notice how much lighter you feel...like you've just dropped a dead weight you didn't know you were carrying, or just discovered the wiper button in your car which, for the first time ever, just cleaned your dirty windshield.

You notice that awareness is absolutely centered, focused and clear.

Well, this changes things, I guess.

J., Tenzin and the gang continue to hover over you like mother hens over a wounded chick.

"Really, I'm fine! Just the heat or exhaustion—from everything. I wasn't drinking enough water...or something," you exclaim.

You are grateful for their concern but are coming around and wish to move on now.

"Okay." J. looks at you questionably and wraps things up with "We'll discuss in the car."

J. notices Lenny around Tenzin's shoulder. "And you, sir, come with me."

Lenny eagerly hops onto J.'s shoulders. "I think Lenny here saved your ass."

You laugh. *"Something like that."*

J. looks around to everyone and announces. "Gentleman, I think it's time."

317

Everyone understands.

You stand, ready yourself, and you all depart. Before leaving the *Carowinds Café,* however, you track down the young man who roused you from unconsciousness to thank him. You do so expressing your gratitude with a bow, which you surmise probably just embarrassed the poor fellow.

You and the *Seven Dragons* gang make your way to the exit gate and walk through the turnstile single file.

Between the car and the amusement park, you turn around to take in the sights and sounds of *Carowinds* one final time. It's a glorious cacophony of screams, rattles, clacks, thumps, music, steel, concrete, and trees.

What a ride, you think.

Damn...what a ride.

You arrive at the Jeep and van and say your goodbyes. J. gives Tenzin a big bear hug and you do the same.

"Until the next time, brothers," J. says and bows.

They all also bow, holding their hands at their hearts and offering big warm smiles. They get in the van, start the engine and depart.

J. places Lenny in his special spot. "I'll drive," he offers in light of recent events.

You hop in the passenger seat and lift the recline lever on your lower right.

J. gets in, starts the engine and pulls away from *Carowinds*.

A good twenty minutes passes before J. finally breaks the silence.

"So—you gonna tell me what really happened back there?"

You take a big breath, find your center, notice awareness with zero effort and declare: *"I met fear."*

"Really?...with a capital F?"

"With a capital F," you say without hesitation.

"And how do you feel right now?"

"Better than ever." Zero hesitation.

"Okay. Wow. Again! Really!? I am impressed," J. throws an admiring smile your way. "Two roller coasters in one day?"

"I hadn't thought of it that way, but yeah! Two frickin' roller coasters in one day."

"Not bad. Not bad at all."

J. looks at you with absolute knowing in his eyes. Several minutes go by in silence again.

You turn and ask:

"So exactly where are we headed now?"

J. looks at you and responds "home" tersely.

"Home—but I thought we..."

"We are. But given the circumstances, specifically your progress with awareness and fear, you need a break."

"A break?" you say with disappointment.

"How long?"

"Six months."

"Six months! But—"

"No buts...trust me. You gotta let this shit cook. Your turkey is stuffed and baked, my friend. You've made some amazing changes in the short time we've been together. Time to let it sit and cool ...before serving."

"A turkey analogy? Really? That's the best you got right now?"

"Okay...that wasn't my best, but regardless. Six months."

"Oh, man," you huff.

You eventually close your eyes and drift off into sleep. J. drives into the night.

It's 2 a.m. when he pulls into your driveway. J. hops out to help you with your things. He walks you to your front porch.

"Fist bump, friend."

"Oh, hell no!" you declare and give him a big hug.

"Oh shit...almost forgot." You then rush back to the Jeep and open the back door.

"Come here, you little bugger."

You grab Lenny and, as best you can, give him a snuggly little hug.

You walk back up the path to your front porch again, but J. has snuck by you and is now in the front seat of the Jeep again. He starts the engine and rolls down the window. He yells out to you:

"Trust me—in six months you'll be ready. I'll meet you here six months to the day at 7 a.m.—Deal?"

"Hell, yeah—deal!" you shout.

And with that, J. drives off into the night.

Well crap, you think as you turn the key to open the front door of your home. You walk in and turn around, hoping to get one last glimpse of that crazy chartreuse Jeep... but it's nowhere in sight.

Six months is a long time. Six months is a short time. But like all time it simply slips by at its own pace, on its own terms, until finally the day arrives...the time arrives... the moment arrives...

You hear the sound of an engine and you know a chartreuse Jeep is pulling into your driveway. A few moments later, you hear a knock at the door.

Excited, you rush downstairs and open the door.

"Good Morning, Sunshine!" you both shout simultaneously, with laughter on your lips and joy in your hearts.

"You ready to finish this thing?" asks J.

"Abso-fucking-lutely," you reply.

"Wait til you see what I have in store for you!" J says with glee.

You respond seriously, but with a twinkle in your eye:

"You know—six months ago that statement would have scared the shit out of me, but today...well, you're gonna have to try a

321

lot harder than that to get a rise outta me, friend. A lot harder than that..."

"I'll try my best!" J. exclaims with a smile. "I'll try my best."

Inside you are excited as a basket of six-week old puppies.

Let the adventure continue...

Let the adventure continue!!

Spiritual Badass Lesson:

One can only do so much of this work before needing a break, or, um—at least a cold six pack of beer. Both, probably better. It's my humble opinion that too much spiritual shit in too short a time ain't healthy for you. You need a break, a pause, a time to—well, do nothing really. Just sit around, work, play and adjust to all the change that you've made—good or bad. But no spiritual shit...except the stuff deeply, simply and automatically integrated.

I don't know if six months is the right amount of pause time for everyone, but that was about the amount of time I usually needed after an intense experience, workshop or retreat. So, here we are…

Okay.

Move along. Book one of your adventure has just ended.

END PART 4

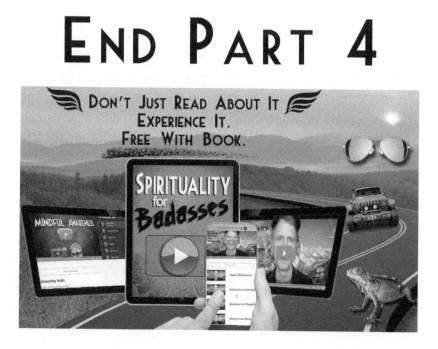

Continue your adventure with J. & Lenny:
Connect, share, laugh, grow & learn
with other books, articles,
videos, courses & more...

Go here:
www.spiritualityforbadasses.com

Thanks to my awesome, smart, loving, funny and spiritual badass family Elisabeth & Jeremy. Thanks to my spiritual badass Mom & Dad. Thanks to my spiritual badass sister Jeanne and her spiritual badass family Ken, Sophie and Charlotte. Thanks to my spiritual badass extended Dixon family in Michigan, Illinois, Colorado and Washington. Thanks to all my spiritual badass best friends- Greg, Miles, Sunny, Darren, Cheryl, Dan, Chuck & Dillon. Thanks to all my spiritual badass teachers (past and present). Thanks to all my great neighborhood friends. Thanks to all my audio visual customers. Thanks to all those spiritual badass online fans who read the early drafts of this book. Thanks to the great god of irreverent, potty-mouthed, spiritual self-help humor. Oh yeah, and of course, thanks to Lenny–you green skinned, little rascal muse you.

I spiritual badass love ya all.

Spirituality for Badasses blossomed out of J. Stewart's life as a spiritual seeker, finder and teacher. He teaches based on his direct experience, twenty-nine years of interaction with numerous nonduality-advaita-zen-unorthodox teachers, his ongoing education / certification in modern mindfulness and a degree in communications/engineering from Syracuse University.

He is a frequent media guest, heard on hundreds of national radio stations, podcasts, vlogs and blogs across the country, in big cities such as Los Angeles, Chicago, Seattle, Boston, and everywhere in between. He has been a featured expert with major media brands such as SiriusXM Radio, iHeart Media, Audacy (formerly Entercom/CBS Radio), Radio America and more.

REVIEWS & SHARING
HELL YES PLEASE!

Your friends will be jealous ...

Your friends will be jealous you discovered this book before they did! They're gonna love it *and* you're gonna get some serious badass friend points. Help get the word out: Review it, share it and recommend it.

Things you can do:

Write a review:
Make your world a more spiritual badass place: After reading, please leave a review with your thoughts and opinions. Just search *Amazon, Kobo, BookBub or Goodreads* for *Spirituality for Badasses* and spread the love baby.

Snap a photo & share:
Snap a photo of you and your copy of the book. Write a few words about it and share it on facebook, twitter, snapchat, etc.

Share your review or photo with me:
Spirituality for Badasses is on facebook. Drop me a line and share your thoughts or photos of you with the book.

Buy an extra copy to give away:
Buy an extra copy and keep it in your car. Save it to give to the perfect person–and change the world, one spiritual badass at a time...

Fist Bump & Thank you!
J. Stewart Dixon

References

Becker, Michael. 1973.
The Denial of Death.
Free Press / Simon & Schuster, Inc.

Washburn, Michael. 1995.
The Ego and The Dynamic Ground.
State University of New York Press, Albany

Welwood, John. 2000.
Toward a Psychology of Awakening
Shambala Publications, Inc.

CPSIA information can be obtained
at www.ICGtesting.com
Printed in the USA
BVHW032252210123
656830BV00004B/74

9 780985 857905